MINECRAFT

First published in Great Britain 2022 by Farshore
An imprint of HarperCollins*Publishers*
1 London Bridge Street, London SE1 9GF
www.farshore.co.uk

HarperCollins*Publishers*
1st Floor, Watermarque Building, Ringsend Road
Dublin 4, Ireland

Illustrations by Ryan Marsh
Special thanks to Sherin Kwan, Alex Wiltshire and Milo Bengtsson

This book is an original creation by Farshore

ISBN 978 0 0084 9599 2
ISBN 978 0 0084 9952 5
Printed in Italy
1

ONLINE SAFETY FOR YOUNGER FANS

Spending time online is great fun! Here are a few simple rules to help younger fans stay safe and keep the internet a great place to spend time:
- Never give out your real name – don't use it as your username.
- Never give out any of your personal details.
- Never tell anybody which school you go to or how old you are.
- Never tell anybody your password except a parent or a guardian.
- Be aware that you must be 13 or over to create an account on many sites. Always check the site policy and ask a parent or guardian for permission before registering.
- Always tell a parent or guardian if something is worrying you.

Stay safe online. Any website addresses listed in this book are correct at the time of going to print. However, Farshore is not responsible for content hosted by third parties. Please be aware that online content can be subject to change and websites can contain content that is unsuitable for children. We advise that all children are supervised when using the internet.

Stay safe online. Farshore is not responsible for content hosted by third parties.

All information and stats are based on Minecraft: Bedrock Edition.

MIX
Paper from responsible sources
FSC™ C007454

MINECRAFT

REDSTONE HANDBOOK

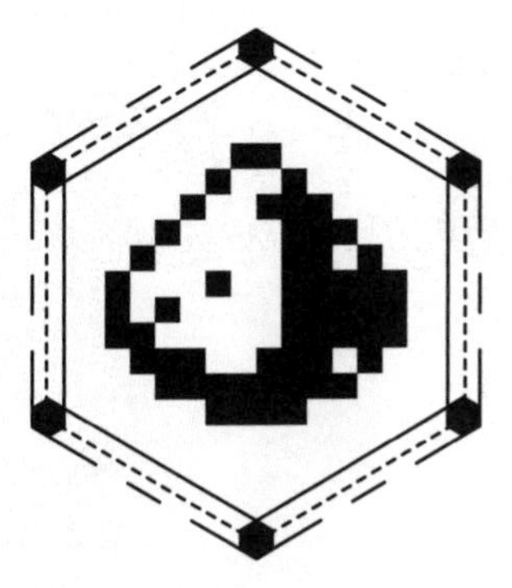

CONTENTS

1. REDSTONE 101

2. PUTTING IT TOGETHER

3. REDSTONE WORKSHOP

WELCOME TO THE MINECRAFT REDSTONE HANDBOOK!

There's always more to explore in the world of Minecraft. Even the bravest defeater of the Ender Dragon, the most intrepid elytra pilot, or mega-city sculptor, may not have yet dug into the incredible depths of redstone.

Learning how to use redstone is your way to building useful contraptions that automate farming, traps to prank your friends with, and even computers that work *inside* the game!

Redstone is amazingly rewarding to play with and as powerful as your imagination, but its NOR gates and comparators can be intimidating to newcomers. So you did the right thing to open this handbook, which will teach you everything you need to know to start your own career as a redstone engineer!

It's split into three sections. The first will introduce you to all the blocks that work with redstone and what they do. In the second, you'll learn how to create the essential redstone structures that are found in many contraptions, from clock circuits to staircases. And in the last, you're going to put all that knowledge into action and build fun contraptions that will impress your friends.

LET'S GET ENGINEERING!

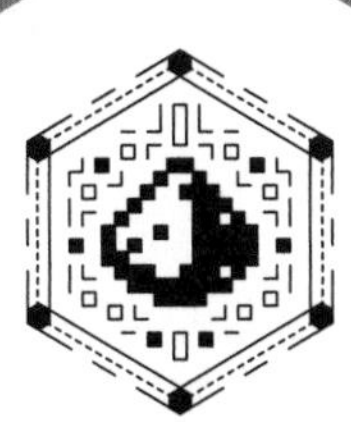

REDSTONE 101

So you're interested in becoming a redstone engineer? Well first thing's first, you need to know all the tools that you will have at your disposal. In this section, you'll be introduced to many of the redstone blocks that will create redstone signals, manipulate them, and use signals to create various useful results.

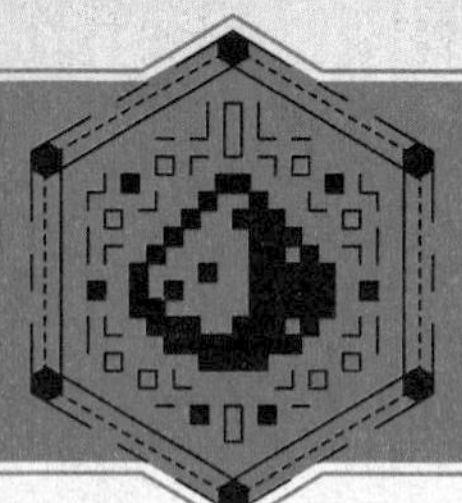

WHAT IS REDSTONE?

WHERE CAN I GET IT?

You can find redstone in its ore form in levels -63 to 15 as normal redstone ore, or the deepslate redstone ore variant if you dig deep enough, but it's most common in the bottom 30 levels. You'll need to use at least an iron pickaxe to mine the ore, which will drop up to five pieces of redstone dust when it's destroyed.

WHAT CAN YOU DO WITH THE DUST?

Everything! If you place dust on top of a block, it will appear as a dark blob. But place a power source, such as a redstone torch, next to it and it will become much brighter, give off particles and carry a signal.

But that's not all, of course. If you place redstone dust on adjacent blocks, they'll join together and reconfigure to carry the signal in up to four directions. Here are just a few of the configurations that you can make.

It's best to look at redstone as the primary conductor of circuits. In its purest form of redstone dust, it can be used to create many components, or transmit a signal between them. If you want to automate any action in Minecraft, redstone is key.

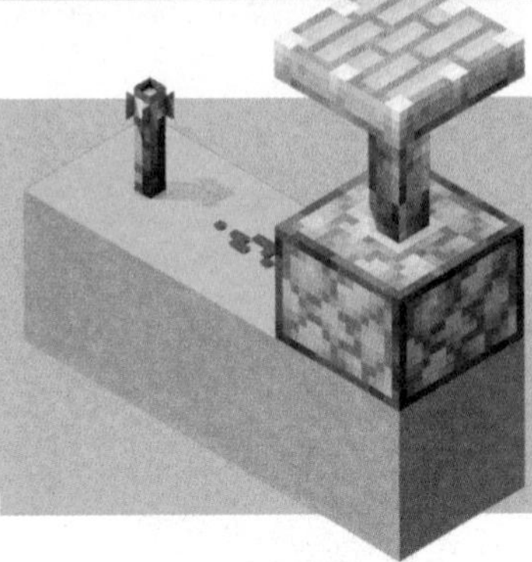

WHAT CAN I DO WITH A REDSTONE SIGNAL?

An active piece of redstone dust will pass a signal on to most adjacent blocks, including normal blocks, as well as those that have a redstone function (see pages 10-13). If a signal is passed to a block that has a function, it will make it perform that task for as long as the signal is present.

SO THERE'S AN ENDLESS POWER SUPPLY?

Not quite. It can last forever, but its strength depends on the source and its distance, which you'll learn more about later. The redstone torch provides the maximum power of 15 to any adjacent redstone dust, but that decreases by 1 for every block it travels across. So a redstone torch can only power redstone dust up to 15 blocks away.

IS THERE ANYTHING ELSE IT CAN DO?

That wasn't enough for you?! Okay fine, redstone dust is also used in recipes to create redstone components such as repeaters, comparators and observers, power sources such as the block of redstone, and daylight detectors, and other clever items such as clocks and compasses. Oh, and it can also be used in brewing to increase the duration of an effect!

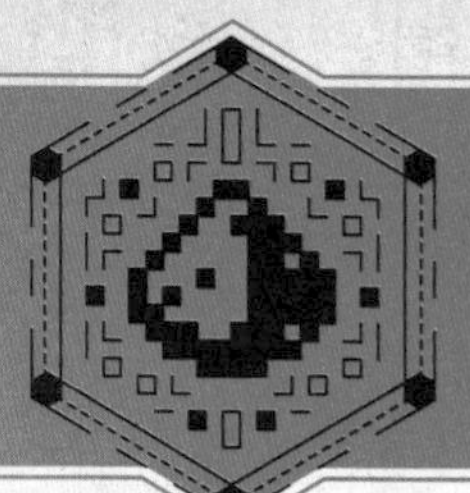

KEY REDSTONE BLOCKS

BLOCK OF REDSTONE

One of the easiest redstone power sources to make is the block of redstone, which can be crafted with 9 pieces of redstone dust. It produces a constant redstone signal to any adjacent space and can never be turned off.

REDSTONE TORCH

Made by crafting a stick with redstone dust, the redstone torch is a useful power source that can be placed on floors and walls. It will turn off if it receives a redstone signal from elsewhere.

LEVER

Levers are useful for when you want to toggle a redstone signal on or off. You can easily switch between both positions – when on, it provides a maximum redstone signal to the block it's attached to.

BUTTON

Press a button to create a temporary redstone signal that will automatically turn off again after a couple of ticks. It can only be activated by players or projectiles, so it is best used as an initial power source.

PRESSURE PLATES

There are four varieties of pressure plates, each with slightly different requirements for activation. All four will produce a constant signal to adjacent blocks while those requirements are met.

Now you know what redstone is, it's time to take a speedy tour of the main blocks you're likely to use in redstone circuits, whether they're providing the power, manipulating the signal or producing an output. Fill your inventory with plenty of these blocks before you read on!

TARGET

The target block produces a redstone signal for a limited time whenever it's hit with a projectile. The closer to the centre that you hit, the stronger the redstone signal will be. Aim for the middle for maximum power!

TRIPWIRE HOOK

Place string between two tripwire hooks, and you'll have a power source that can be activated simply by walking through it. The string is very hard to see, so it is most often deployed in traps.

TRAPPED CHEST

Almost identical to the normal chest, a trapped chest is only recognisable by the dull red glow surrounding its clasp. When opened, it will produce a redstone signal to adjacent blocks until it is closed again.

DAYLIGHT DETECTOR

Powered by natural light, the daylight detector produces a signal with a strength that depends on the time of day and the weather. It can be inverted so that it is powered only in the absence of the sun, too.

REDSTONE REPEATER

The repeater amplifies a redstone signal to its maximum strength of 15, allowing a circuit to travel farther from its power source. It also controls the flow of signals as it only passes one through its front face.

REDSTONE COMPARATOR

A comparator can measure the strengths of up to three signals, or subtract them from one another. It's also used to determine the fullness of storage blocks and even how many slices of a cake are remaining.

PISTON

With the power to push many blocks, the piston is often used in redstone circuits to create moving mechanisms. When activated by a redstone signal, it extends its head into the block facing it.

STICKY PISTON

In addition to pushing blocks, the sticky piston can pull some, too. There are exceptions that might break or are immovable, such as obsidian, but the sticky piston offers a new dimension to circuits.

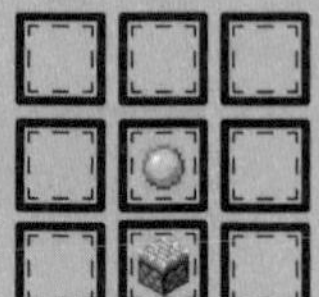

DISPENSER

You can store items in a dispenser, however, when it receives a redstone signal, it will eject its contents, sometimes activating their function, such as shooting an arrow or launching a splash potion.

DROPPER

Just like the dispenser, the dropper is a storage block that ejects items when it's powered, but it never activates them, making it the safest way to move items around a circuit.

HOPPER

The most versatile storage block is the hopper. They can feed items from one container to another, and will collect items that fall on top of them, making them an important part of many redstone builds.

OBSERVER

This straight-faced block constantly checks the block space directly in front of it and produces a redstone signal from its rear face when it observes a change. It can spot a range of different block changes.

SCULK SENSOR

While the observer detects mostly visible changes, the sculk sensor does similar for vibrations. It outputs a differing signal for events, from footsteps to the opening of a chest.

TOP TIP

Sculk sensors can only be mined, or looted from a chest. Find them in the deep dark biome.

DETECTOR RAIL

The detector rail is a variant of rail that carries minecarts and produces a redstone signal when a minecart rolls over it. It can be used with the activator and powered rails to create complex rail systems.

ACTIVATOR RAIL

Minecarts travel on set paths of activator rails as normal. When they are powered by redstone, any carts that roll over them will be activated, causing hopper minecarts to move items or the TNT minecart to explode!

POWERED RAIL

When receiving a redstone signal, the powered rail can activate others around it on a minecart track. When activated, it will increase the speed of a minecart, however, it will slow its speed if it's inactive.

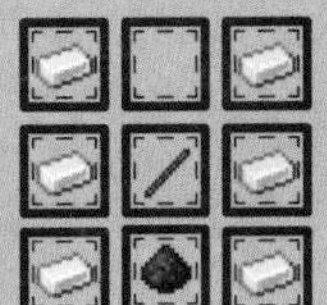

REDSTONE LAMP

The only dedicated redstone light source is the redstone lamp, crafted with redstone dust and glowstone. Unlike glowstone, the redstone lamp can be toggled on and off when it receives a redstone signal.

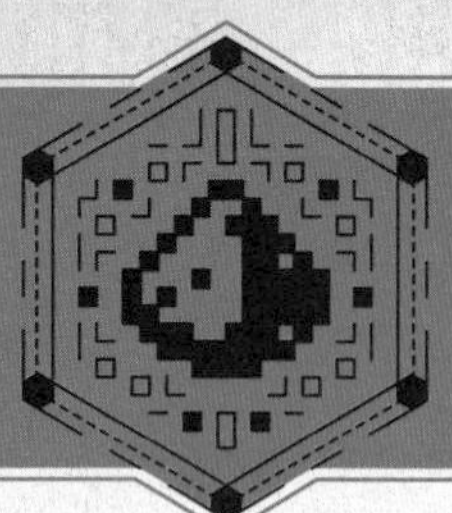

REDSTONE POWER

REDSTONE TORCH

Placed on its own, the redstone torch produces a constant redstone signal at maximum strength to blocks that are horizontally adjacent to or above the torch. Redstone torches are turned on by default, which makes them great for powering redstone lamps. But be warned – when it receives another power or signal, its signal is inverted.

BLOCK OF REDSTONE

When it is placed, a block of redstone produces a constant, maximum strength signal to blocks beside any of its faces. Unlike the redstone torch, you can not invert its signal, but by using pistons and sticky pistons you can move it, so it is possible to use it in a toggled power system. You can craft one using 9 redstone dust.

LEVER

Interact with a lever and it will produce a continuous redstone signal at maximum strength until it is interacted with again. Use one to open a door and it will remain open until you turn the lever off. Mobs can not interact with levers, so they're great home security.

To make any redstone contraption work, you need to use one of the various power blocks. Each one has a slightly different way of working, which means there's always one that's perfect for your build. Let's take a closer look at these bright sparks.

BUTTON

When pressed, the button will produce a temporary maximum signal to the block it's attached to or adjacent components, before switching back off again, which is known as monostability. It will open a door briefly, letting you walk through, but will close the door behind you to prevent undesirable visitors.

DAYLIGHT DETECTOR

When a daylight detector is exposed to natural light, it will output a variable signal to adjacent components depending on how bright the light is. Because of this, you can use it to create automatic night lights that turn on as soon as it gets dark outside. A great way to keep your base safe.

TARGET

The target block outputs a monostable redstone signal when hit by a projectile – the closer it gets to the centre of a face, the stronger the signal, while arrows and tridents double the duration. It can also be used to alter the path of redstone, though any redstone signal it receives has no effect on the target.

PRESSURE PLATES

There are four types of pressure plates, all activated in some fashion by weight being placed on top of them and deactivating when the weight is removed.

Wooden pressure plates always produce the maximum signal strength, whether it's a player, mob or item that's on top of it.

Stone pressure plates produce the same maximum signal as wooden plates, but only work with players and mobs.

Light weighted pressure plates produce a variable signal depending on how many players, mobs or items are on them – 15 will produce the max signal.

The heavy weighted variant behaves identically to the light version, but requires ten times the amount of entities.

TRAPPED CHESTS

While you can store items in it, the trapped chest will power adjacent redstone components when open. The signal strength it produces corresponds to how many people are accessing it, up to a maximum of 15. As it's a storage block, its contents can be measured by comparators and output a signal based on how full it is. The signal will turn off once the chest is closed.

TRIPWIRE HOOKS

Place a pair of tripwire hooks on solid blocks facing each other and run string between them to create a tripwire. When a player or mob walks through the tripwire, it will create a monostable signal at the maximum strength at each tripwire hook, which can be handy for initiating several components of a contraption, such as an intruder alarm or even automated arrows.

OBSERVER

An observer monitors a block directly in front of it and outputs a maximum monostable signal whenever the observed block changes. For instance, it can detect when an item is rotated in a frame, or whether a crop such as sugar cane has grown. Once it notices a change, it will send a signal from its rear, opposite the block it's observing.

SCULK SENSOR

The sculk sensor detects vibrations in a nine-block radius, and outputs a monostable signal that is stronger when the vibrations are closer. The signal it produces is wireless, meaning it doesn't need to be directly connected to redstone components in order to activate them. However, this can trigger unexpected parts of larger contraptions if you're not careful. You can use a redstone comparator to produce a traditional redstone signal based on the type of vibration the sculk sensor detects.

GETTING INTO REDSTONE WITH: JIGARBOV

WHAT INFLUENCED YOU TO EXPLORE REDSTONE?

'I have always been interested in making games for people to play, but never been really good at programming. There have been a number of game-making games before, but Minecraft's ease of world editing and redstone capability, coupled with its now very comprehensive command block syntax, has allowed me to pursue my dream of actually making games for people to play as a career on the Minecraft Marketplace. It all started when I began playing around with redstone in a big sandstone world and seeing the potential of what was possible.'

WHAT ATTRACTED YOU TO REDSTONE OVER CREATIVE BUILDING?

'What I love the most about redstone is how you create things that can manipulate the world around you, much like any tool but more indirectly. While I am not the best creative builder, what redstone allows me to do is to tell a story for players in a more dynamic manner than just in a static world.'

At first glance, redstone can seem like a mindbogglingly complicated series of systems, so we talked to master redstone engineer, YouTube star and Marketplace creator Jigarbov to find out exactly how he made his first strides in the tricky world of redstone.

WHAT HAVE YOU DONE WITH REDSTONE?

ITEMS BY JIGARBOV PRODUCTIONS

SEE FULL CATALOG

'Learning redstone has allowed me to make a whole host of interactive experiences, games, puzzles and other maps for players to play. You can even move on to command blocks and coding and doing it professionally on the Minecraft Marketplace.'

WHAT DO YOU LIKE MOST ABOUT REDSTONE?

'The thing I like most about redstone is its adherence to logical rules. Do this, then this happens. The transition from that kind of logic to coding is a surprisingly small step to make, the difference obviously is that you go from placing dust and torches to writing it as code.'

WHAT DO YOU LOOK FORWARD TO WITH REDSTONE?

'Every redstone addition is very exciting, including the sculk sensor, which will allow previously unsupported mechanics to be added, such as wireless redstone.'

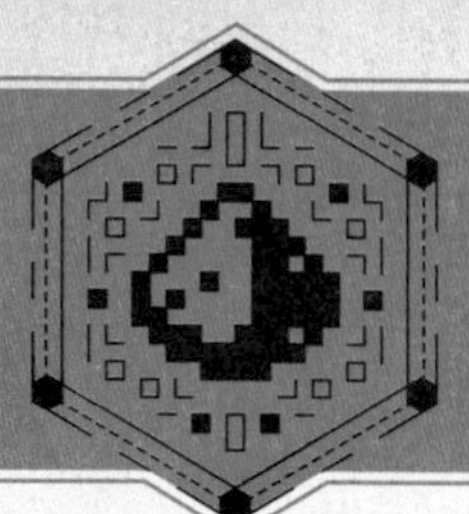

MOVERS AND SHAKERS

REDSTONE REPEATER

The redstone repeater is used to control the flow of a signal and restore its strength to the max. Redstone only flows one way from a repeater, represented by the arrow on top. If a repeater receives a signal into the side from another repeater, it will lock the output as either on or off. You can edit the repeaters to add a delay to the signal – the farther apart the mini torches are, the longer the delay.

PISTON

When a piston receives a redstone signal, it extends its head into the block space it faces, moving any block in the direction of the extension. It can push up to twelve blocks in a row, including any that are joined by slime or honey blocks. Some blocks are resistant to pushing, such as lodestones, while others will break instead of being moved, such as pumpkins.

STICKY PISTON

The head of the sticky piston is covered in slime, which allows it to pull most blocks that can be pushed, too. They can be used for ingenious contraptions, such as a retractable drawbridge over a lava moat!

HOPPER

You can manipulate items from storage with a hopper, which is a very precise way to move items around. It has an output tube that can be altered to face the sides of blocks, or directly down, depending on where you want to send the items. The open top is used to collect loose items, but it can also pull items out of storage and sort them directly to another chest.

What good is a redstone signal if it doesn't actually do anything? That's where this bevy of blocks come in. Each one has some way of manipulating signals, items or blocks, which can be used as the end point of a contraption, or another cog in your genius machine.

DROPPER

Droppers have storage slots and will drop a single item whenever a redstone signal is received. They can be activated by a signal coming from any direction and can be placed so that the output face points in all six directions. If there is more than one type of item in its storage, it will randomly pick an item to eject. Unlike the dispenser below, a dropper will never activate items.

DISPENSER

The dispenser releases any items in its storage slots whenever it receives a redstone signal. Like the dropper, it will only drop one item per activation, so it needs to be placed in a circuit that activates over and over to emit more than one item. Some items that a dispenser emits will have activated effects – arrows, eggs and snowballs will be fired, armour will be equipped on a passing player or mob, while TNT and firework rockets will be triggered!

REDSTONE COMPARATOR

Comparators are multi-purpose blocks. They flow signals in a single direction like repeaters and can also measure the contents of storage items to output a variable signal strength based on how full the storage is. They have two main modes – comparison and subtraction.

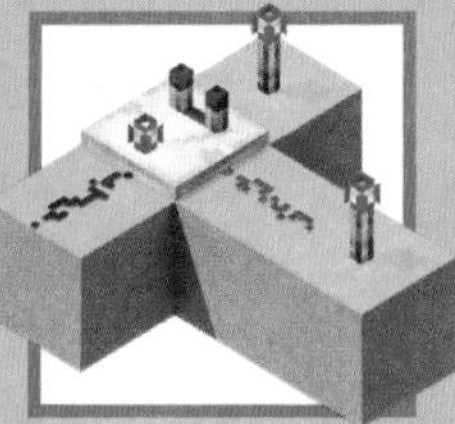

In subtraction mode, the strongest side signal is subtracted from the one entering the block from the back. So if the strongest side signal is 3 and there is a back signal of 10, a signal with a strength of 7 will be output. If the side signal is greater than the back signal, nothing will be output.

In comparison mode, the front mini torch is unlit and the comparator will compare the strength of signals entering its side to the one in the rear. If the rear signal is greater than both side signals, it will be passed through the front, otherwise it won't output anything.

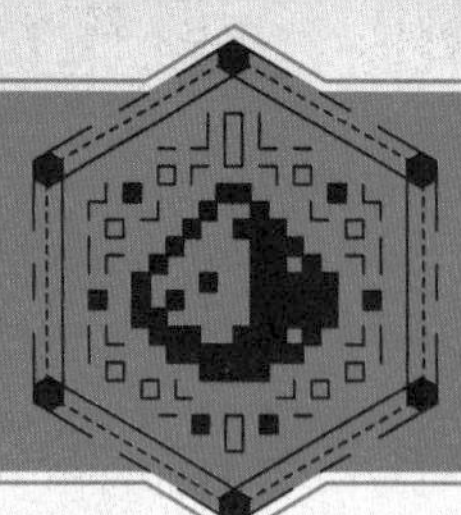

REDSTONE RAIL

RAIL

Normal rails are used to create tracks along with the redstone-infused variants. They connect in similar ways to redstone dust in order to create curves, T-junctions and crossroads, as well as ramps. T-junctions and crossroads can be toggled by a power source to change the direction of travel.

POWERED RAIL

If you want to accelerate minecarts around a track, you need the powered rail, which must be activated with a detector rail or another power source. Using the power of redstone, you can send minecarts up slopes and even create your own fun rides or roller coasters.

DETECTOR RAIL

The detector rail is the only rail-based power source, and can activate redstone rails, as well as other redstone components. It will produce a maximum strength signal when a minecart rolls over it. If a comparator is placed beside a detector rail, it produces a variable signal for passing minecarts with chests and hoppers, depending on how full they are.

Who says that redstone contraptions have to stay still? With the inclusion of rails, you can take redstone on the road (well, tracks), which opens up a whole new world of function and possibility. Let's look at how to turn simple rails into incredible redstone rides ...

ACTIVATOR RAIL

If a basic minecart, minecart with TNT or minecart with hopper runs over an activator rail when they are powered, it will cause the minecart to eject mobs or players, begin the ignition of the TNT or disable a hopper from picking up items. Conversely, if a hopper minecart passes over an inactive detector rail, it will begin to pick items up again.

MINECARTS

Now you have a cool redstone track, what are you going to run on it? Here are all the carts at your disposal:

MINECART

The basic minecart can carry one player or mob and has no function other than being able to initiate activator rails.

MINECART WITH CHEST

A minecart with a chest carries the same amount as a normal chest. The more it contains, the quicker it slows down.

MINECART WITH FURNACE

The locomotive of minecarts – feed it fuel to make it move around the track, even without a redstone push.

MINECART WITH HOPPER

A minecart with hopper hoovers up nearby items or pulls items out of storage blocks they run underneath.

MINECART WITH TNT

A volatile cart that blows up if it takes a corner too fast. Primed by activator rails and often used in explosive mining.

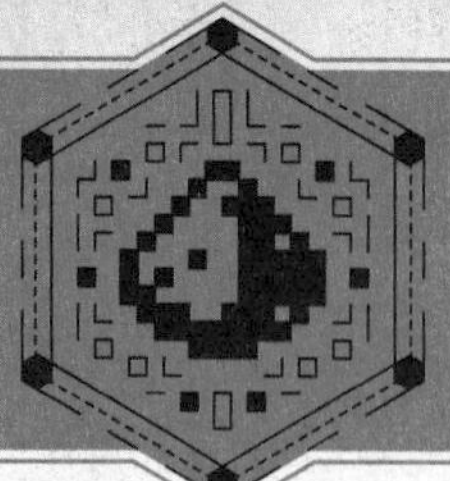

REDSTONE TOOLBOX

GLAZED TERRACOTTA

A clever building block to start with is glazed terracotta. Not only are the patterns great for separating different mechanisms within a contraption, they're also unique in that they can be pushed by pistons, but not pulled by sticky pistons.

SLIME BLOCK

The stickiness of the slime block can be used in conjunction with pistons and sticky pistons to push blocks that aren't directly in front of a piston head, as long as the connected blocks don't total more than 12. Most mobs will bounce off slime blocks, but items won't.

HONEY BLOCK

Like slime, honey blocks will also try to move adjacent blocks when they're pushed by either type of piston, but items, players and mobs will remain stuck to the block. When players and mobs try to move off the block, they are only able to do so slowly.

TNT

Incorporated into many builds from mining mechs to arrow cannons, TNT is an explosive block that can be primed by redstone and many of the redstone blocks. It's often combined with pistons and slime to bounce it away from the redstone contraption that spawns it.

OBSIDIAN

If you can't launch TNT away from your contraption, obsidian is the go-to block to protect the most important parts of your circuits. It has one of the highest blast resistances in the game, which can protect from almost any explosion, including TNT, fireballs and creeper blasts, as well as resist the flows of water and lava. However, it's completely immovable when placed.

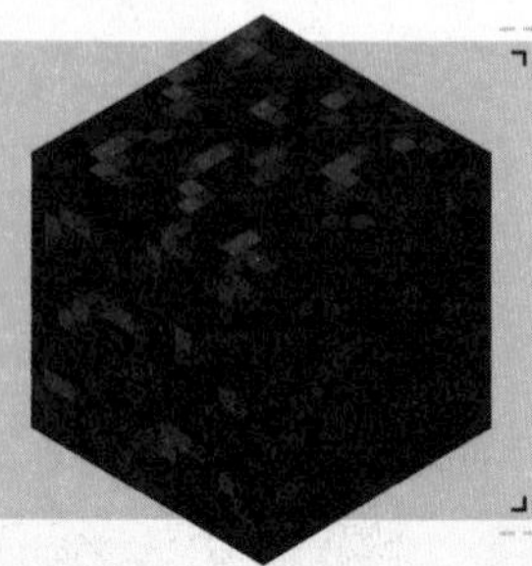

Of course, you can't just use redstone blocks to build contraptions. It would be chaos! Beyond making structures from your normal building blocks, there are a few special blocks that complement the behaviour of redstone blocks perfectly. Let's see what they are!

ANCIENT DEBRIS

So you want the durability of obsidian, but you also want it to move? Well ancient debris has got you covered. Unlike obsidian, it can be pushed and pulled by pistons and sticky pistons, which means you can have very moveable, very resistant elements in your build.

SLABS

These half-height blocks, available in over 50 different styles, are useful when creating compact vertical redstone. Rather than creating a spiral of redstone dust travelling up or down (see page 32), you can place them in 'ladder' formations in a 1x2 space to make your redstone more compact. However, they must occupy the top half of the block space.

ITEM FRAMES

Many items can be measured by comparators to create a variable redstone signal, but the easiest one to master is the item frame. Place one on a block in front of a comparator, and it will let you choose a signal strength based on the orientation of the item inside!

NOTE BLOCKS

Redstone can be used to activate note blocks. These can be used as alarms, or arranged in routes to play compositions. You can alter the pitch by interacting with it, and change the instrument – everything from a flute to a didgeridoo – by swapping the block it's sitting on.

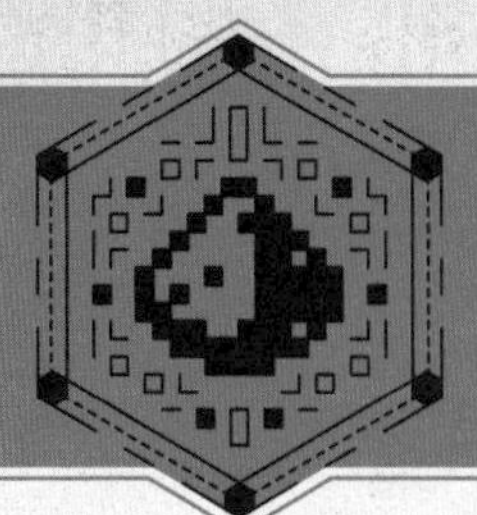

TROUBLESHOOTING

GET CREATIVE

You don't need the added strife of trying to ward off creepers that might blow up your partially built circuits, so when you first build a contraption, do it in Creative mode. It's the best place to practise without worrying about mobs, health or hunger, so you can focus solely on getting your redstone right.

USE COLOUR BLOCKS

Using a simple block such as terracotta in the structure for your mechanisms will make all the redstone elements stand out nicely. When you get to more complicated builds, you can separate out different parts of your contraption with a different colour of terracotta, so you can easily pinpoint errors.

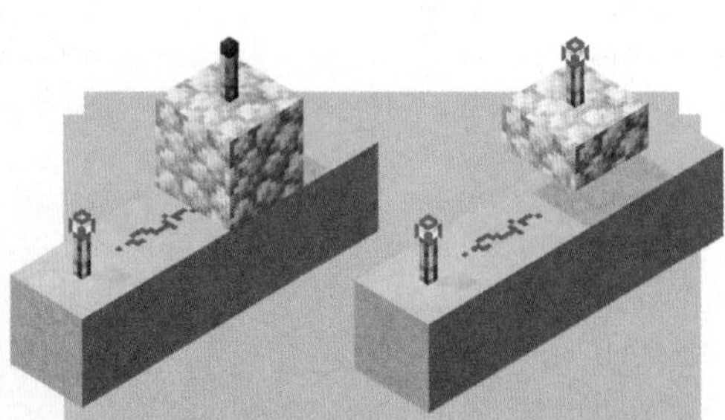

NOT CLEAR AT ALL

There are some partial blocks and some transparent ones that can transmit a redstone signal, but in most cases it's easier to use full, opaque blocks to transmit redstone. Whether it's to pass on a signal from a button, or just run redstone dust along, solid blocks are the safest option to begin with. Partial blocks are best used for compact builds.

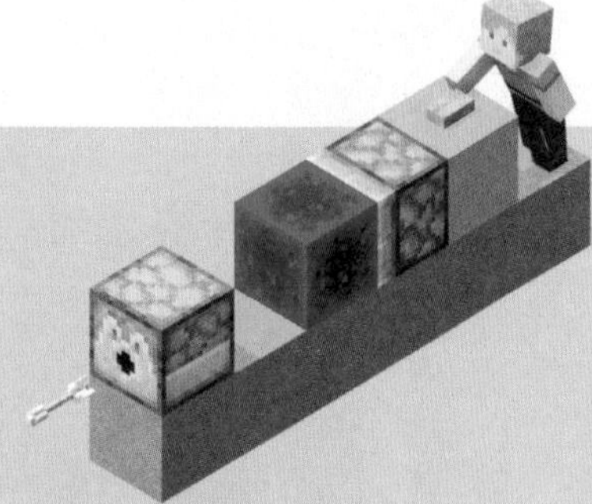

TEST REGULARLY

Don't spend hours building a redstone mechanism without testing it – you might find that you press a button to start it up ... and nothing happens. Instead, make sure you test it every few minutes to make sure all the parts are working as they should, before moving on to the next bit. It's a lot less annoying when something doesn't work.

Redstone is a complicated system, and sometimes trying to make contraptions will leave you frustrated. But don't fear – even the best builders can struggle with it. This selection of handy hints should help you iron out any creases in your new master build.

MAKE IT WORK, THEN IMPROVE

You might see builders trying to make redstone builds as small or as fast as possible, or completely silent. While those are nice things to have, focus on making your build work first of all. Once you have a working contraption, you can consider parts that you might be able to make smaller, or bits that could work more efficiently by using some different mechanism choices.

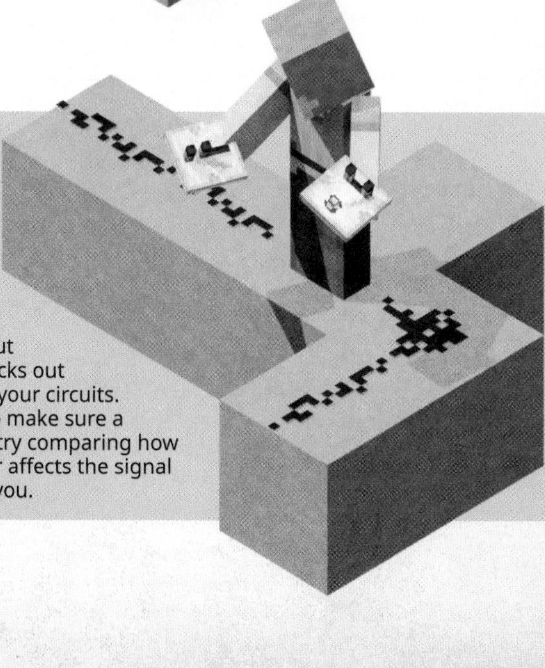

REPLACE BLOCKS

The toolset for redstone is huge and the possible interactions between them is a tangled web. You might think that you know exactly how you want your build to work, but don't be afraid to swap blocks out to see how they behave in your circuits. For instance, if you want to make sure a signal only flows one way, try comparing how a comparator or a repeater affects the signal and which one is right for you.

PUTTING IT TOGETHER

Now you've learned the basics and filled your inventory with all the redstone components you might need, it's time to look at how they can be combined to achieve amazing things. In this section, you'll discover all the different circuits you can use and how to combine them to build simple contraptions – and then some epic larger builds!

REDSTONE RECIPES

INVERTED SIGNAL

By adding a redstone torch to the front of a solid block, you can invert a signal that enters the rear of the block. So basically the front torch is only powered on when the main power source is off. This is particularly useful when you want to switch the purpose of a lever, button or pressure plate.

VERTICAL INVERSION

You can also invert a signal vertically by stacking redstone torches and solid blocks alternately. It works in exactly the same way, but passes a signal upwards. The only niggle with this is that you need to have an odd number of redstone torches to invert a signal, otherwise it will match the input.

SLIMY PISTON

Not a sticky piston, but a piston with a slime block attached to it. Rather than only being able to push and pull a block that is on the front face of a slime piston, a slime block attached to a piston will allow you to push and pull blocks attached to all five exposed faces. You can also use a honey block in the same way.

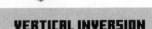

Before we dive into learning about circuits, it might be wise to look at a few helpful combos that you'll find in some of the upcoming builds. You may be able to use these nuggets of wisdom in other circuits and contraptions beyond what we'll see later on, too.

FLOW CONTROL

Repeaters, as well as being able to maximise a redstone signal, are great at controlling the flow of redstone circuits. They'll take a signal from the block that sits beside them and only pass it out the front, allowing you to have wires running beside each other.

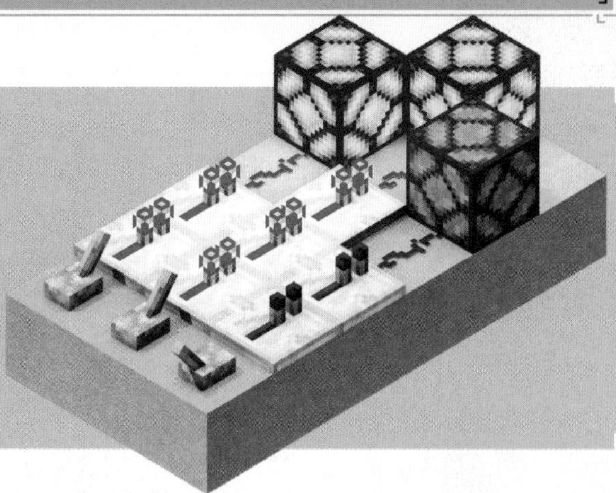

SLAB CIRCUITRY

Slabs are a unique tool in redstone because they are only half a block in size, but can still have redstone dust on top of them. They're very useful for controlling the flow of redstone vertically because they will pass a signal up, but not down, similar to a repeater's ability to control horizontal flows.

MEASURING CONTENTS

The comparator's main functions are to subtract and compare signals, but it can also measure the state of blocks and produce a signal accordingly. It can measure the fullness of any block with storage slots, such as chests and dispensers, as well as a beehive, bee nest, cake, cauldron, composter, command block, end portal frame, item frame, jukebox, lectern, respawn anchor and sculk sensor.

VERTICAL TRANSMISSION

STAIRCASE

This vertical transmission circuit can pass a redstone signal up or down, but can take up a lot of space, especially if you need to wrap it around other elements.

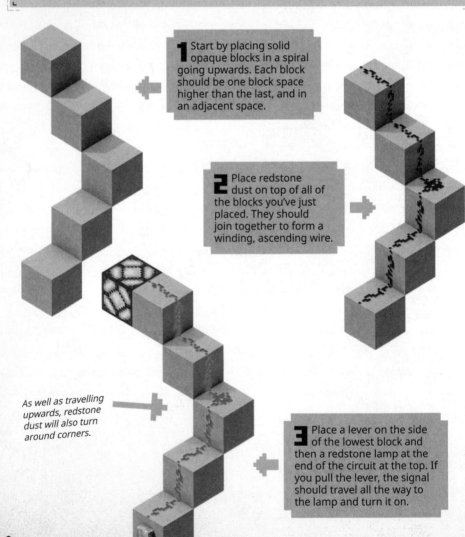

1 Start by placing solid opaque blocks in a spiral going upwards. Each block should be one block space higher than the last, and in an adjacent space.

2 Place redstone dust on top of all of the blocks you've just placed. They should join together to form a winding, ascending wire.

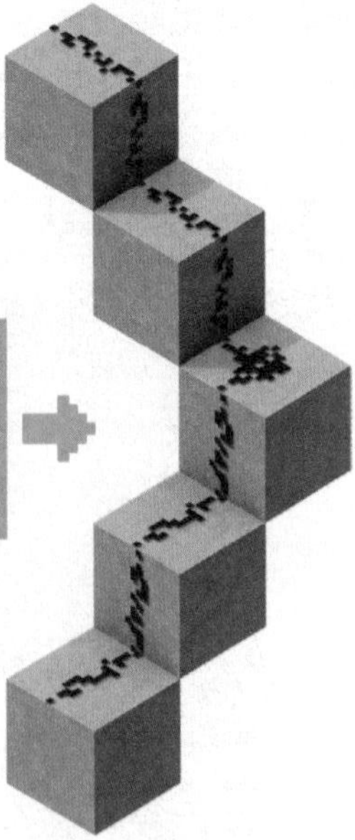

As well as travelling upwards, redstone dust will also turn around corners.

3 Place a lever on the side of the lowest block and then a redstone lamp at the end of the circuit at the top. If you pull the lever, the signal should travel all the way to the lamp and turn it on.

Now it's time to put everything you've learnt into practice and build your first circuit. We're going to start easy, with a vertical transmission circuit that can pass a signal from the ground upwards – useful for controlling mechanisms that need to be far above or below a switch.

LADDER

This version is much more compact, requiring only a 1x2 space on the ground, however, it can only pass a redstone signal up, not down.

1 Build two columns out of any solid block. Leaving a two-block space between the two columns.

2 Add a slab beside the lowest block on one of the columns. It should occupy the top half of the block space, so place it against the top half of the block.

3 Do the same thing on the opposite column. Add a slab against the top half of the second block. Repeat this alternation, until you reach the desired height.

4 Destroy the solid blocks, except the one that the lowest slab is placed on. Put redstone dust on each slab. You'll notice that it doesn't join into a wire.

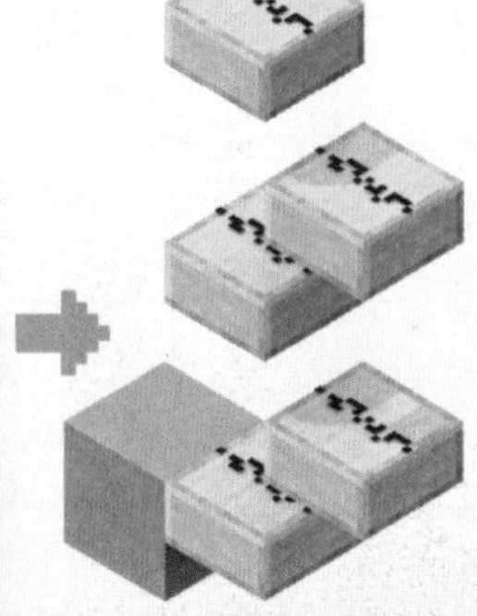

5 Place a lever on the solid block, and a redstone lamp beside the highest slab. Pull the lever and the signal will pass up the ladder and turn the lamp on.

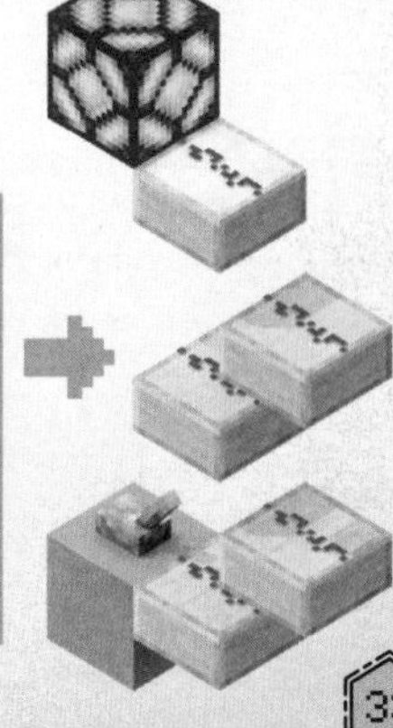

INTRUDER ALARM

DIFFICULTY:

30 mins

MAIN BLOCKS

FRONT

SIDE

TOP

Why don't we use your new redstone skills to make a contraption with vertical redstone? This intruder alarm uses both the staircase and ladder vertical transmissions to let you know when invaders try to enter your base and will even aim to fend them off, too!

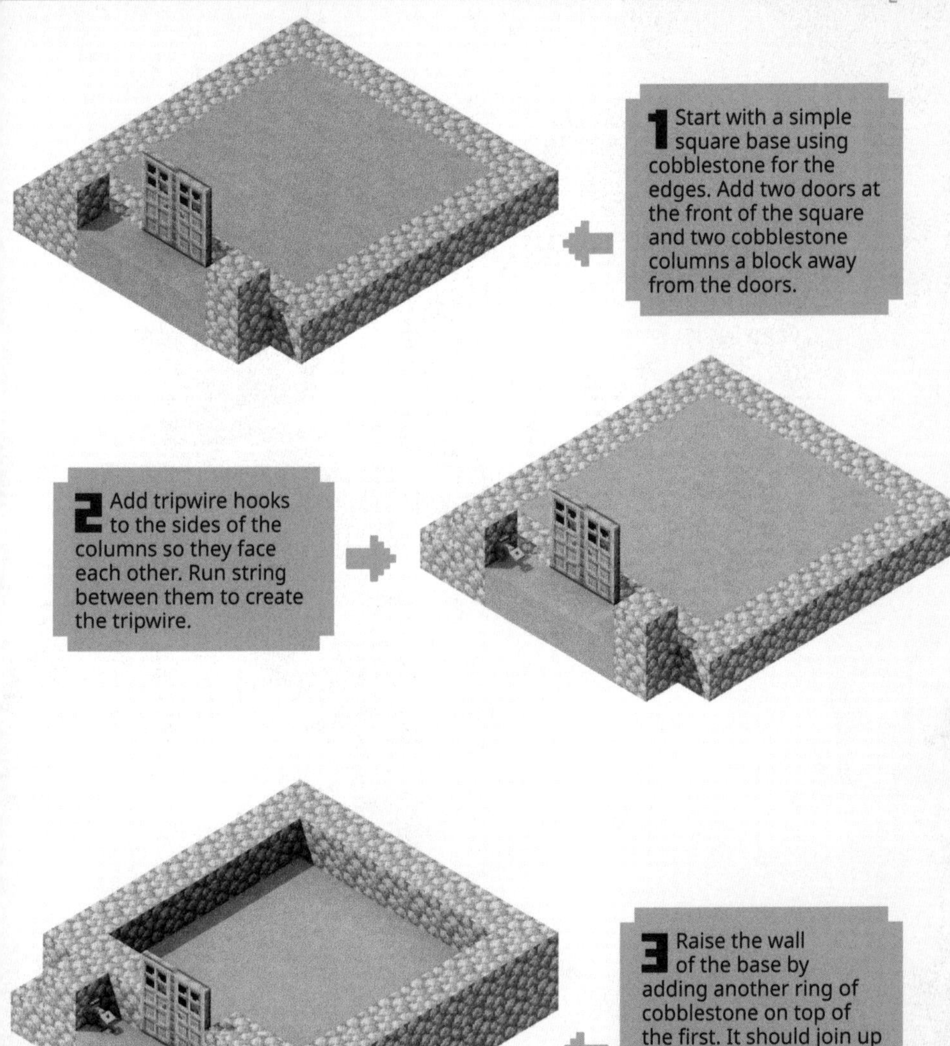

1 Start with a simple square base using cobblestone for the edges. Add two doors at the front of the square and two cobblestone columns a block away from the doors.

2 Add tripwire hooks to the sides of the columns so they face each other. Run string between them to create the tripwire.

3 Raise the wall of the base by adding another ring of cobblestone on top of the first. It should join up level with the columns you placed in the first step, but leave a gap behind the two doors.

4 Add redstone dust from the cobblestone behind the left tripwire's block to halfway down one of the side walls as shown.

5 From this redstone, we'll create the ladder. Place some blocks to build a temporary wall, then add slabs in an alternating pattern until it reaches the desired height. Add redstone dust on each slab.

6 From the top of the ladder, build a row of 4 solid blocks out across the middle of your build. Place redstone dust on the first, a repeater on the second, and then two note blocks on the final 2 blocks. The repeater will boost the redstone signal so that it reaches the note blocks.

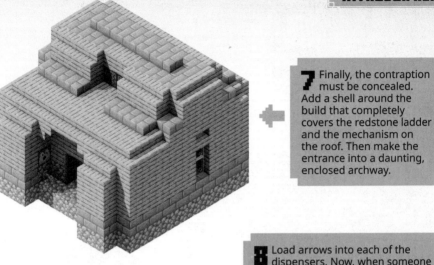

7 Finally, the contraption must be concealed. Add a shell around the build that completely covers the redstone ladder and the mechanism on the roof. Then make the entrance into a daunting, enclosed archway.

8 Load arrows into each of the dispensers. Now, when someone steps through the tripwire, the alarm on the top of the building will go off and arrows will shoot at whoever is standing at the door.

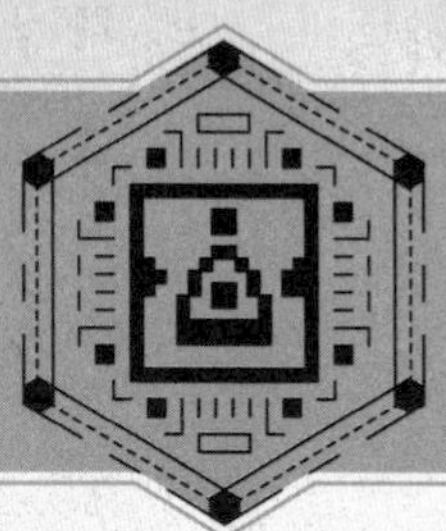

LOGIC GATES

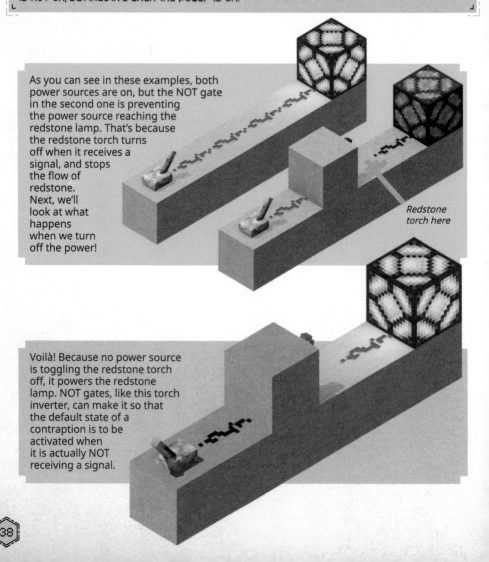

NOT GATE

The first logic gate we're looking at is called a NOT gate. By default, a redstone component will activate when its power source is on, but by adding a NOT gate between the source and the component, the component will be activated when the power source is NOT on, but inactive when the power is on.

As you can see in these examples, both power sources are on, but the NOT gate in the second one is preventing the power source reaching the redstone lamp. That's because the redstone torch turns off when it receives a signal, and stops the flow of redstone. Next, we'll look at what happens when we turn off the power!

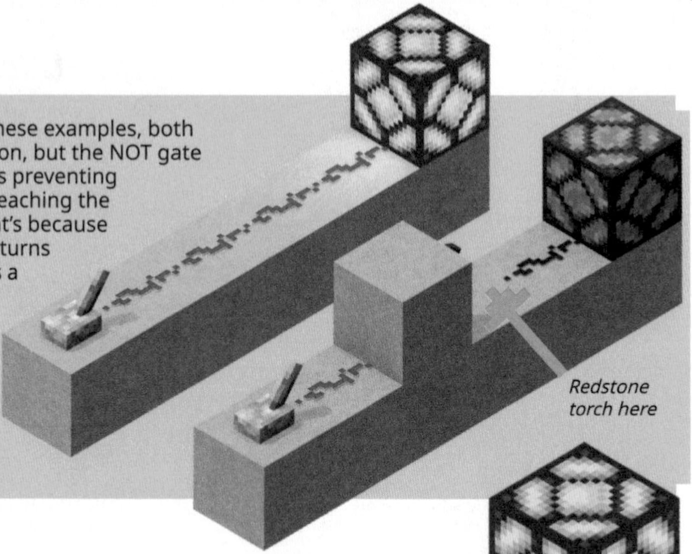

Redstone torch here

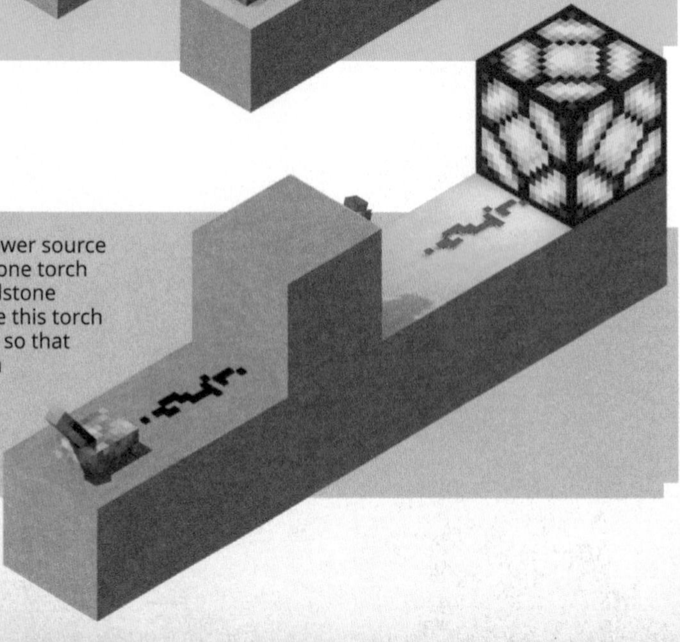

Voilà! Because no power source is toggling the redstone torch off, it powers the redstone lamp. NOT gates, like this torch inverter, can make it so that the default state of a contraption is to be activated when it is actually NOT receiving a signal.

As well as being able to send a signal up and down, there are also circuits that control IF a signal should be sent at all. Logic gates can be set up to sort one or more signals and provide an output when certain criteria are met. Let's take a look at a few very useful gates.

OR GATE

If you want to enable multiple inputs to a redstone contraption, you have several choices. Using an OR gate will pass on a redstone signal when either input is on. The example below uses three different inputs that travel through redstone repeaters to isolate the signals.

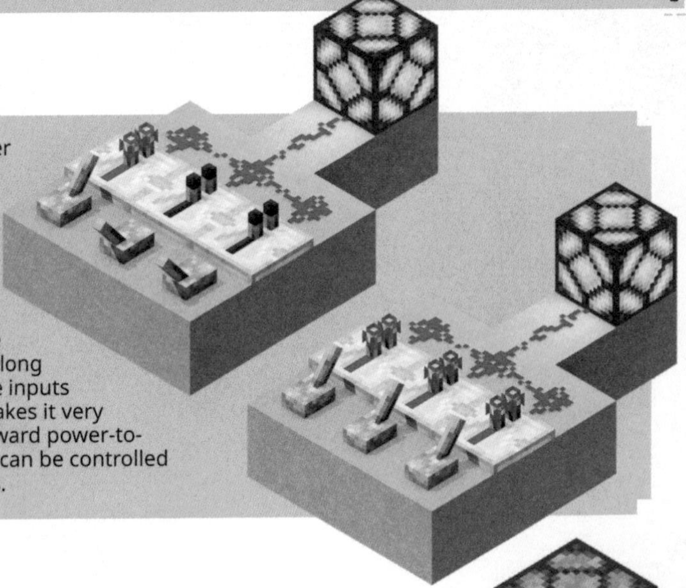

In this example, if either the first OR the second OR the third lever is activated, the redstone dust behind all the inputs will remain active and power the redstone lamp. The lamp will remain on as long as one, two or all of the inputs are activated, which makes it very similar to a straightforward power-to-output setup, except it can be controlled from multiple locations.

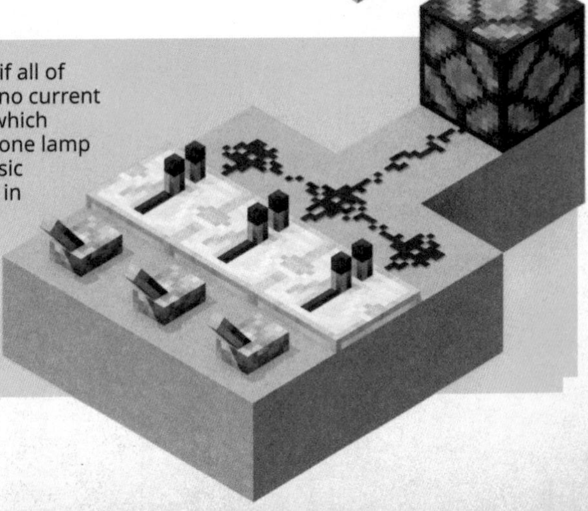

The OR gate won't be powered if all of the levers are inactive because no current is reaching the redstone dust, which turns off the signal to the redstone lamp and renders it inactive. It's a basic principle, but when formulated in this way with multiple inputs, it is a useful logic gate that can form the base of others (such as the NOR gate on the next page) or keep several inputs separate while performing the same function.

NOR GATE

We can combine the NOT gate and the OR gate to make a logic gate that will only pass on a signal when none of the inputs are active. If we add the torch inverter mechanism from the NOT gate to the OR gate, you'll create a NOR gate.

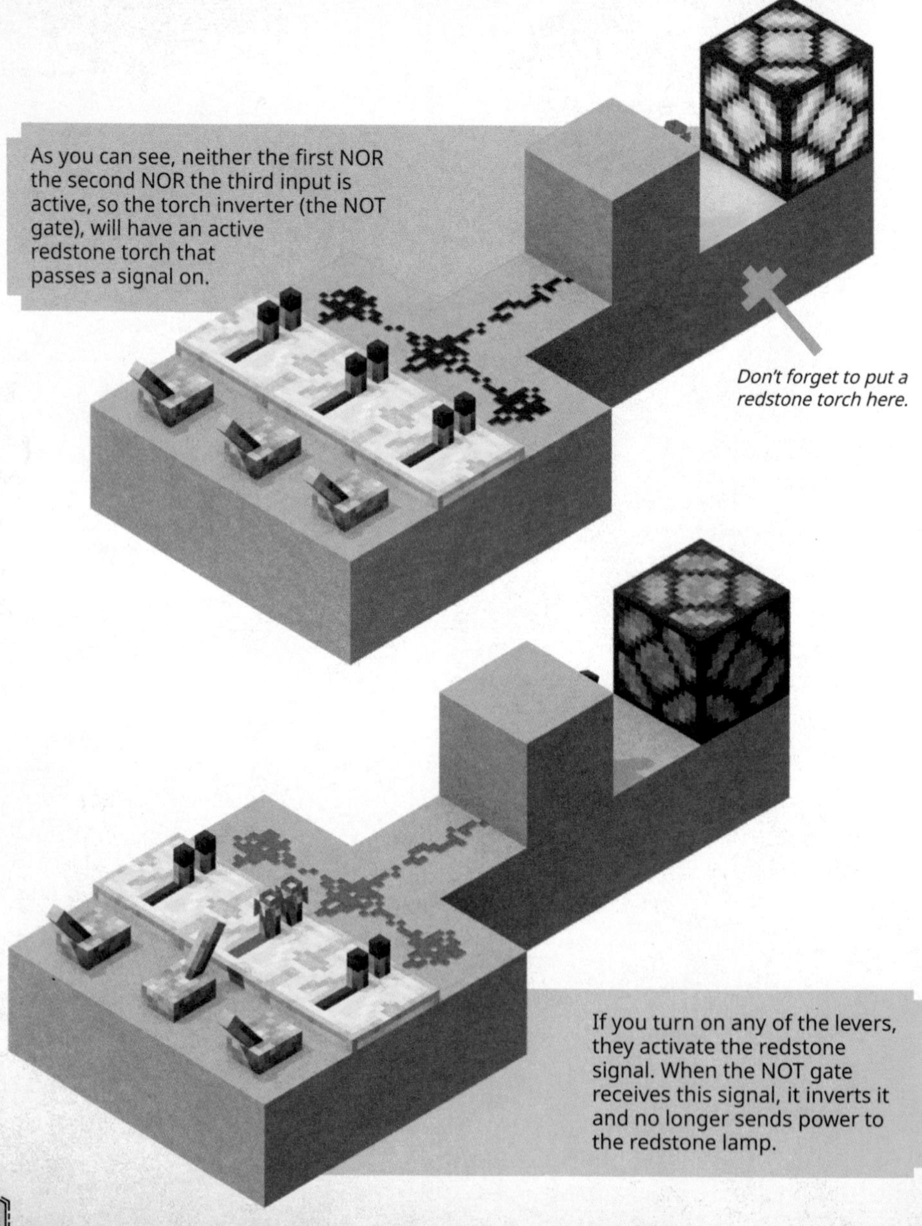

As you can see, neither the first NOR the second NOR the third input is active, so the torch inverter (the NOT gate), will have an active redstone torch that passes a signal on.

Don't forget to put a redstone torch here.

If you turn on any of the levers, they activate the redstone signal. When the NOT gate receives this signal, it inverts it and no longer sends power to the redstone lamp.

AND GATE

Finally we have the AND gate, which will pass on a signal only when all of the component inputs are active. This example shows an AND gate with two different input sources that flow into redstone torches. If both the inputs are inactive, the redstone torches will remain on, which power the redstone dust in between them and keeps the final redstone torch inactive.

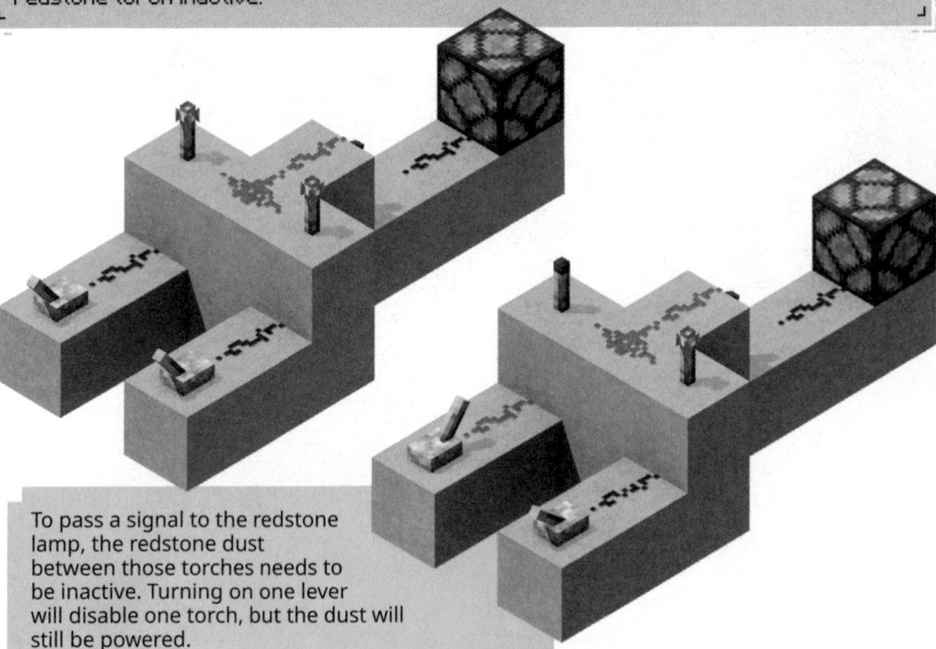

To pass a signal to the redstone lamp, the redstone dust between those torches needs to be inactive. Turning on one lever will disable one torch, but the dust will still be powered.

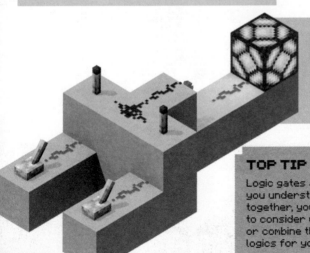

By making the second input inactive, both torches will be disabled along with the redstone dust, which powers the final torch and passes a signal along the circuit.

TOP TIP

Logic gates are easily expanded. If you understand the way they're put together, you can extend each of them to consider with even more inputs, or combine them to create different logics for your contraptions.

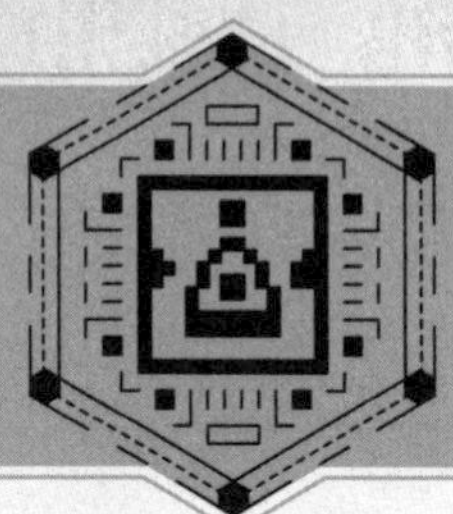

SHOOTING GALLERY

DIFFICULTY:

35 mins

MAIN BLOCKS

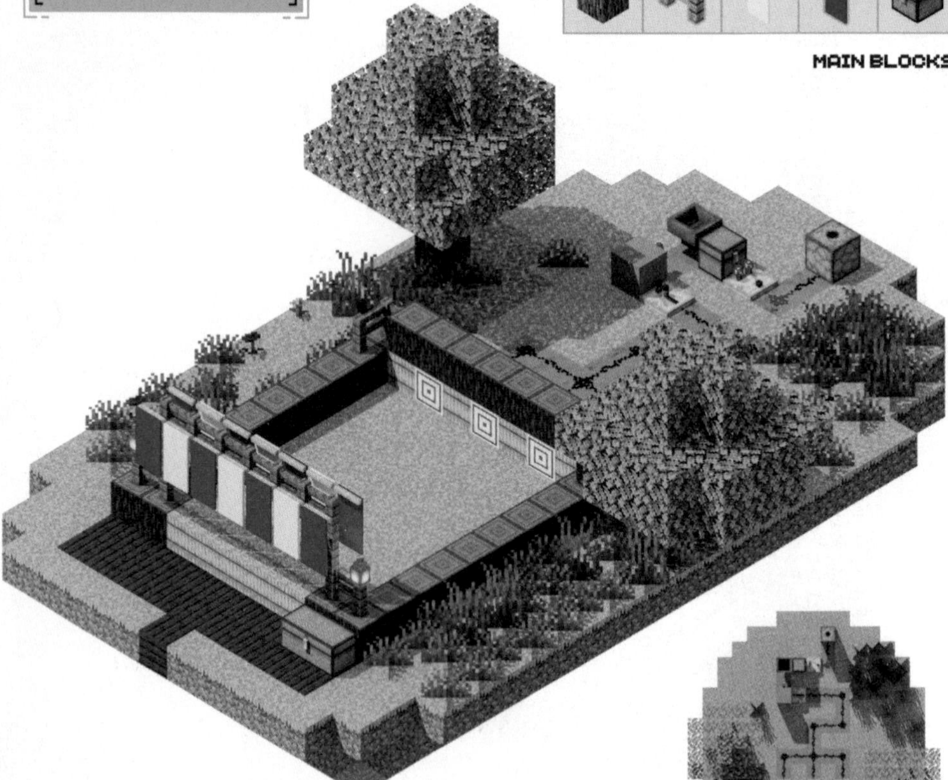

FRONT

SIDE

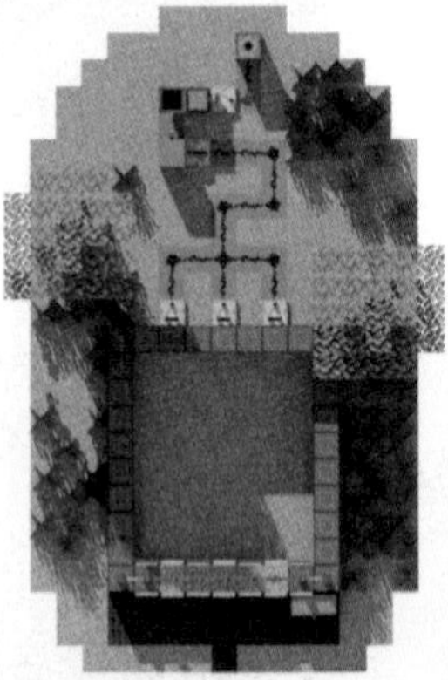

TOP

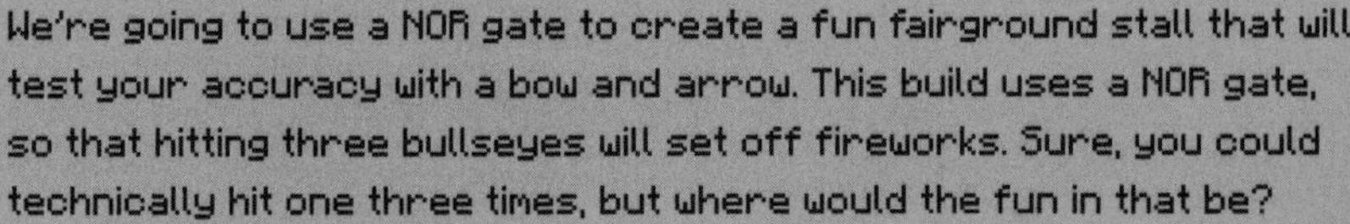

We're going to use a NOR gate to create a fun fairground stall that will test your accuracy with a bow and arrow. This build uses a NOR gate, so that hitting three bullseyes will set off fireworks. Sure, you could technically hit one three times, but where would the fun in that be?

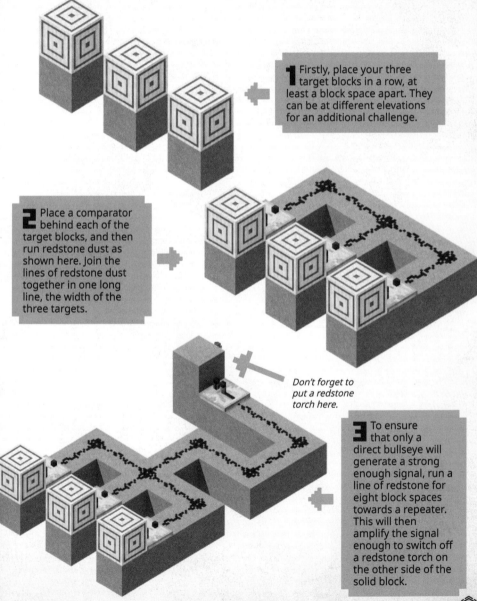

1 Firstly, place your three target blocks in a row, at least a block space apart. They can be at different elevations for an additional challenge.

2 Place a comparator behind each of the target blocks, and then run redstone dust as shown here. Join the lines of redstone dust together in one long line, the width of the three targets.

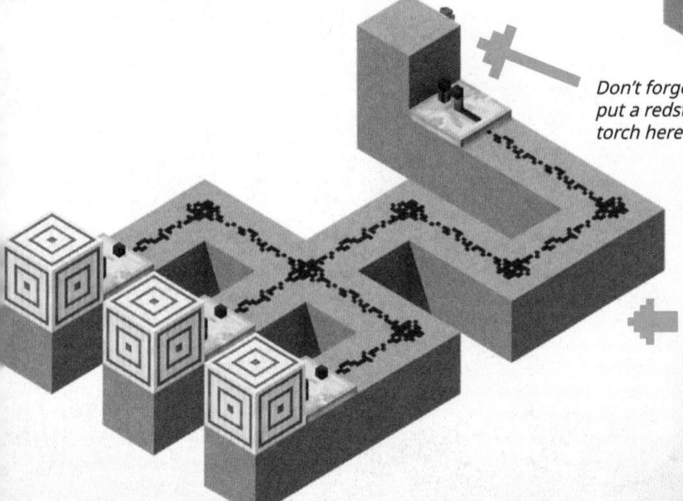

Don't forget to put a redstone torch here.

3 To ensure that only a direct bullseye will generate a strong enough signal, run a line of redstone for eight block spaces towards a repeater. This will then amplify the signal enough to switch off a redstone torch on the other side of the solid block.

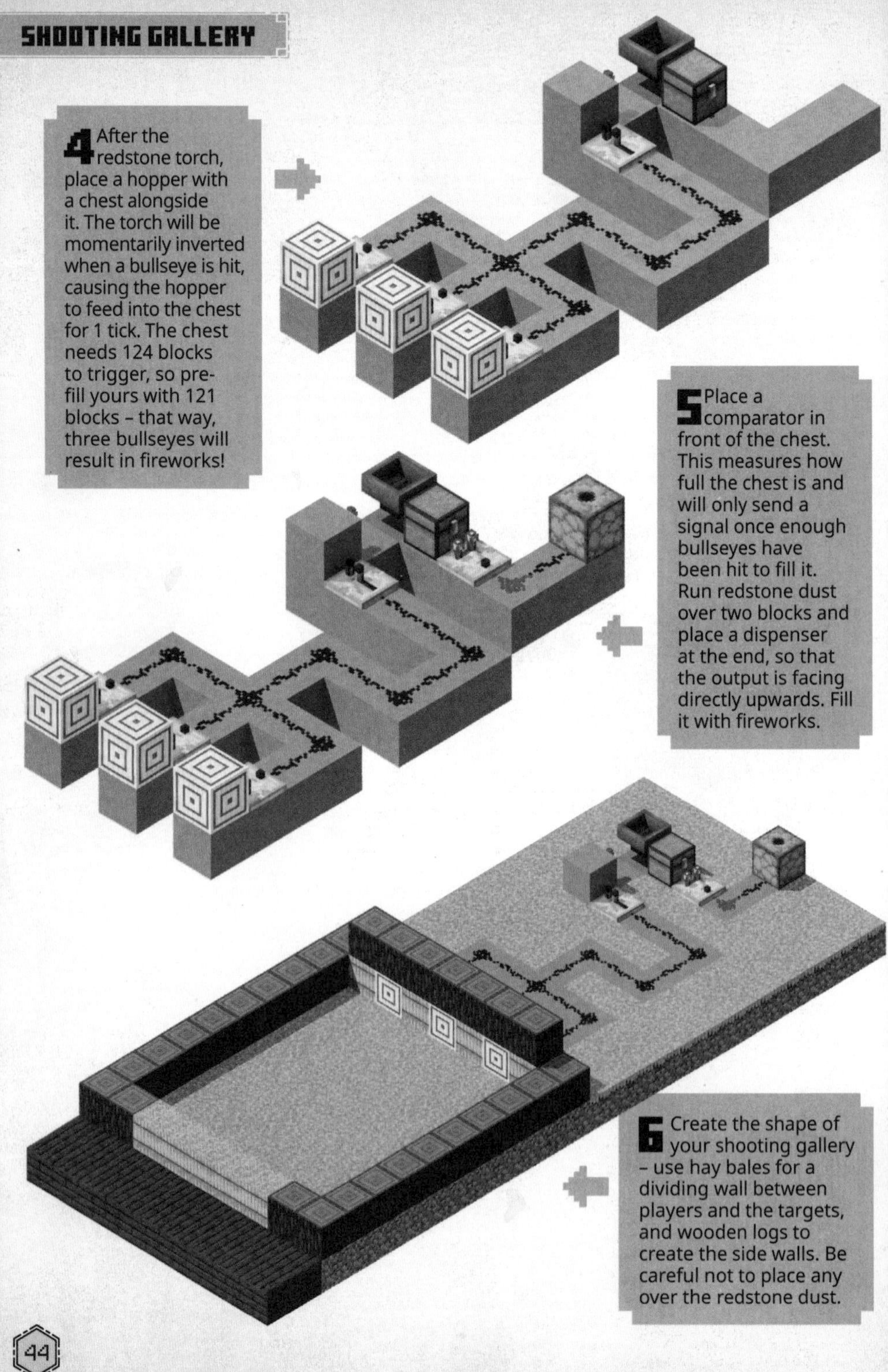

4 After the redstone torch, place a hopper with a chest alongside it. The torch will be momentarily inverted when a bullseye is hit, causing the hopper to feed into the chest for 1 tick. The chest needs 124 blocks to trigger, so pre-fill yours with 121 blocks – that way, three bullseyes will result in fireworks!

5 Place a comparator in front of the chest. This measures how full the chest is and will only send a signal once enough bullseyes have been hit to fill it. Run redstone dust over two blocks and place a dispenser at the end, so that the output is facing directly upwards. Fill it with fireworks.

6 Create the shape of your shooting gallery – use hay bales for a dividing wall between players and the targets, and wooden logs to create the side walls. Be careful not to place any over the redstone dust.

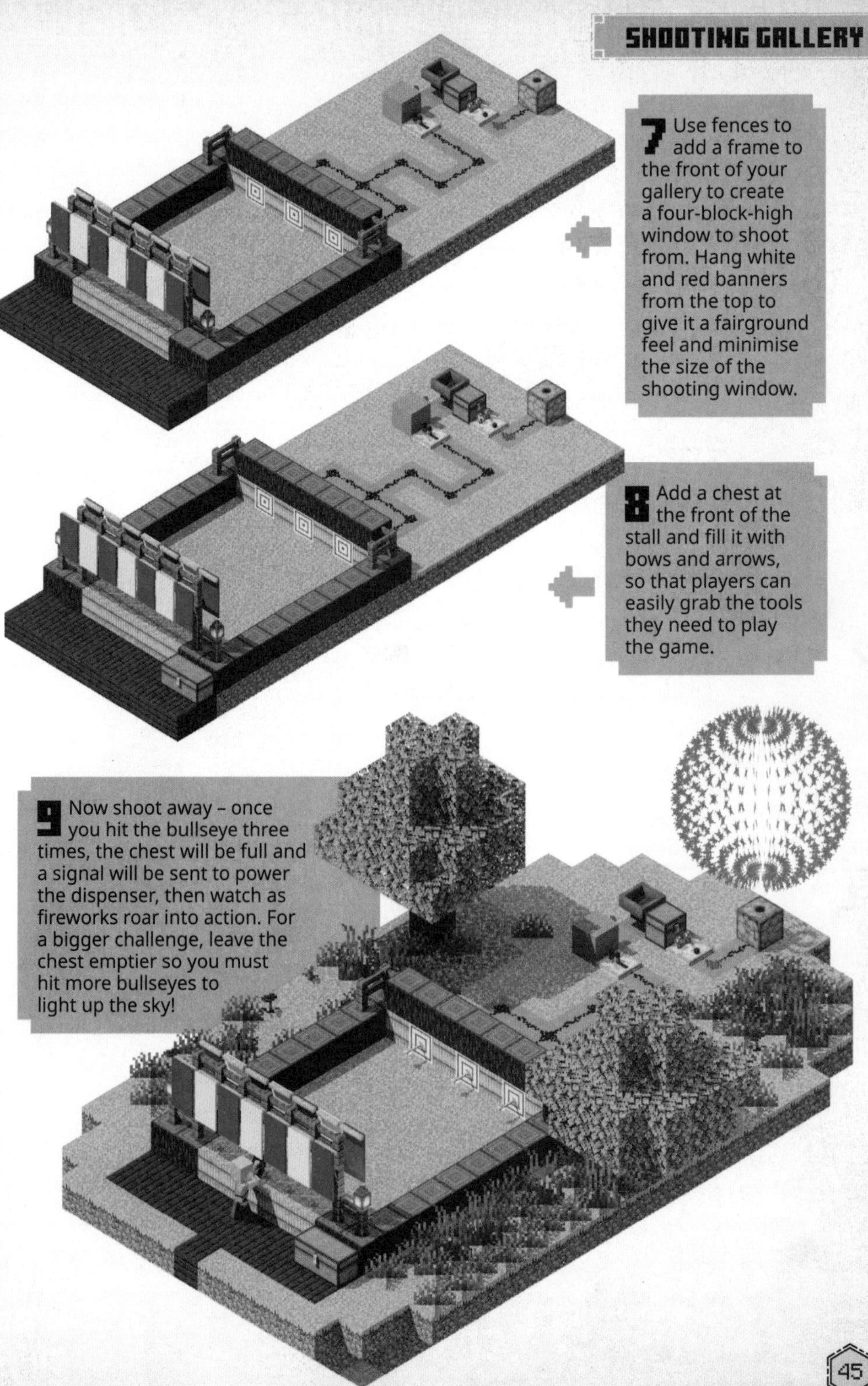

7 Use fences to add a frame to the front of your gallery to create a four-block-high window to shoot from. Hang white and red banners from the top to give it a fairground feel and minimise the size of the shooting window.

8 Add a chest at the front of the stall and fill it with bows and arrows, so that players can easily grab the tools they need to play the game.

9 Now shoot away – once you hit the bullseye three times, the chest will be full and a signal will be sent to power the dispenser, then watch as fireworks roar into action. For a bigger challenge, leave the chest emptier so you must hit more bullseyes to light up the sky!

PULSE CIRCUITS

PULSE GENERATOR

To create a pulse signal, you'll need a generator. The easiest way to create a generator is to combine 3 repeaters with a lever and redstone dust. When a lever is activated, it will power the first 2 repeaters. The first (set to 2 redstone ticks) passes its signal onto the redstone dust, while the other locks the third repeater, holding the signal at the redstone dust. Now, when you switch the lever off, the first two repeaters deactivate, which unlocks the third repeater and allows the signal to flow, briefly lighting the redstone lamp.

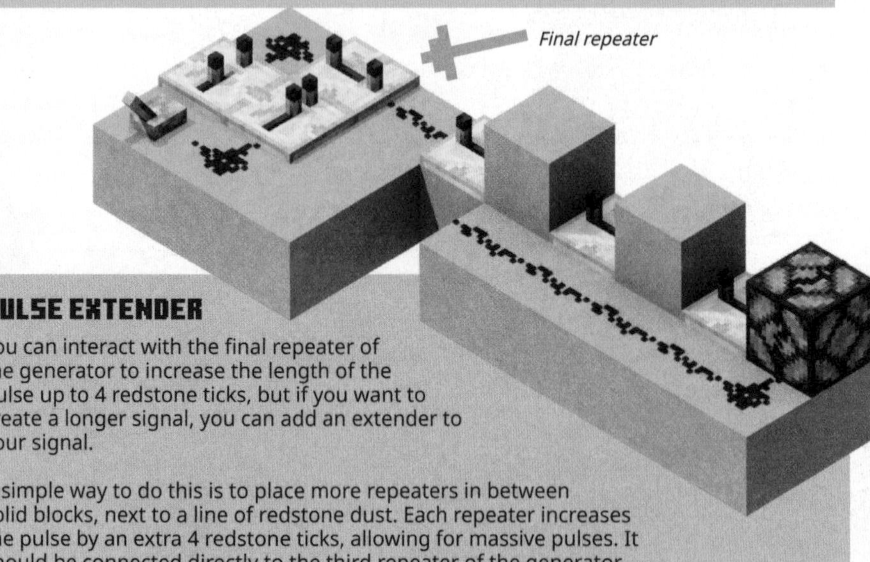

PULSE EXTENDER

You can interact with the final repeater of the generator to increase the length of the pulse up to 4 redstone ticks, but if you want to create a longer signal, you can add an extender to your signal.

A simple way to do this is to place more repeaters in between solid blocks, next to a line of redstone dust. Each repeater increases the pulse by an extra 4 redstone ticks, allowing for massive pulses. It should be connected directly to the third repeater of the generator.

Various redstone items generate a pulse in Minecraft, such as buttons, but pulse circuits offer you a way of creating the same burst of redstone signal with more control over its behaviour. Let's look at how to make a pulse circuit and how to adapt its signal, too.

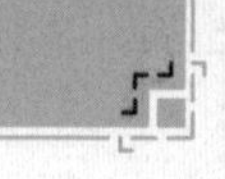

PULSE LIMITER

If your pulse stays powered for too long, you can use a limiter to reduce its length. Start with a generator, but this time connect it to a limiter, composed of a piston and solid blocks. When the pulse reaches the highest solid block, it powers the repeater for a single tick, as well as the piston beneath it, which will stop the rest of the pulse going anywhere.

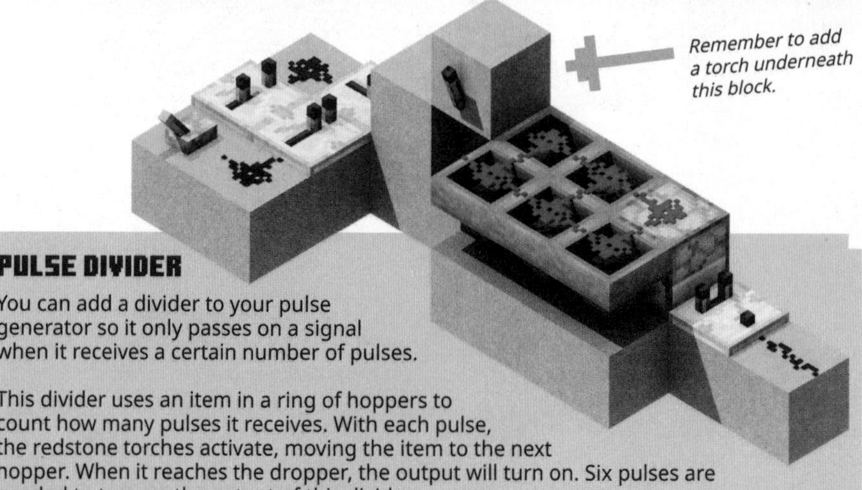
Remember to add a torch underneath this block.

PULSE DIVIDER

You can add a divider to your pulse generator so it only passes on a signal when it receives a certain number of pulses.

This divider uses an item in a ring of hoppers to count how many pulses it receives. With each pulse, the redstone torches activate, moving the item to the next hopper. When it reaches the dropper, the output will turn on. Six pulses are needed to turn on the output of this divider.

DID YOU KNOW?

Minecraft operates on a looping process known as a tick. Redstone ticks are comprised of 2 game ticks, which equates to 0.1 seconds. The pulse generator creates a pulse that lasts 1 redstone tick, so it will pass through each block in 0.1 seconds. The extenders and limiters are used to increase and decrease the length of a pulse to multiple ticks.

HIDDEN STAIRCASE

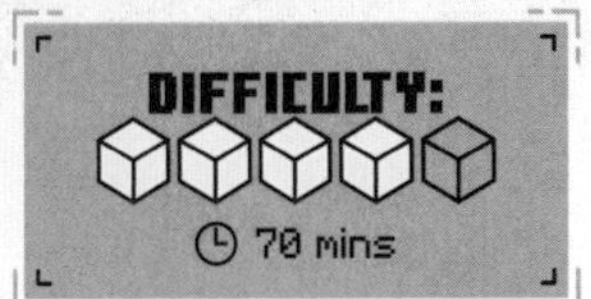

MAIN BLOCKS

FRONT

SIDE

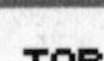

TOP

Pulse circuits are great for making a change to something in Minecraft for a brief amount of time before reverting it. For instance, it's perfect for hiding a staircase in your base to protect hidden floors. Follow these steps to build your own secret staircase wall in your base.

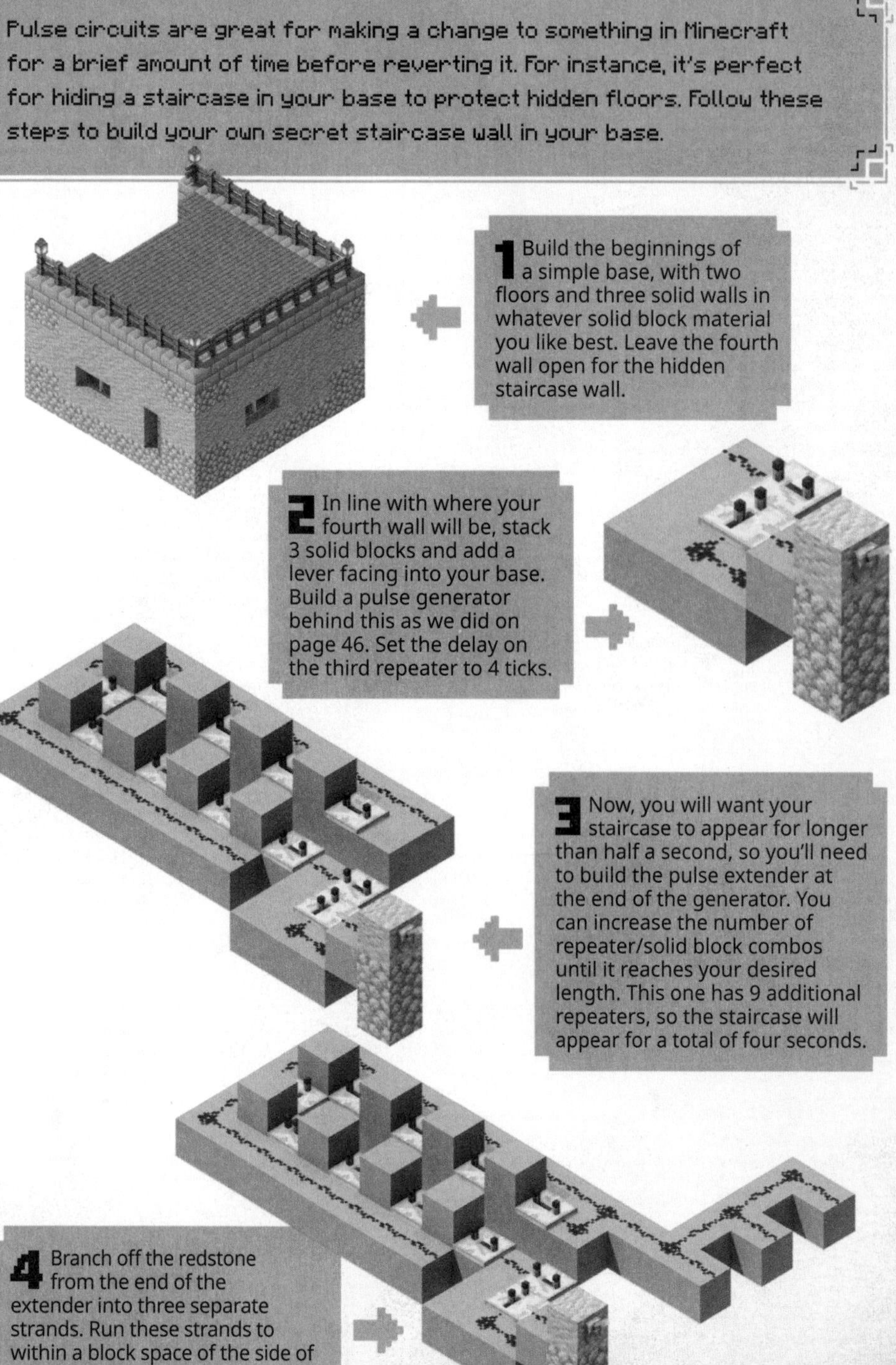

1 Build the beginnings of a simple base, with two floors and three solid walls in whatever solid block material you like best. Leave the fourth wall open for the hidden staircase wall.

2 In line with where your fourth wall will be, stack 3 solid blocks and add a lever facing into your base. Build a pulse generator behind this as we did on page 46. Set the delay on the third repeater to 4 ticks.

3 Now, you will want your staircase to appear for longer than half a second, so you'll need to build the pulse extender at the end of the generator. You can increase the number of repeater/solid block combos until it reaches your desired length. This one has 9 additional repeaters, so the staircase will appear for a total of four seconds.

4 Branch off the redstone from the end of the extender into three separate strands. Run these strands to within a block space of the side of your base that has no wall.

5 Add three solid-block pillars one block away from where you want your wall to be. These need to cascade in size so that each one is two blocks taller than the last, forming a base for your staircase.

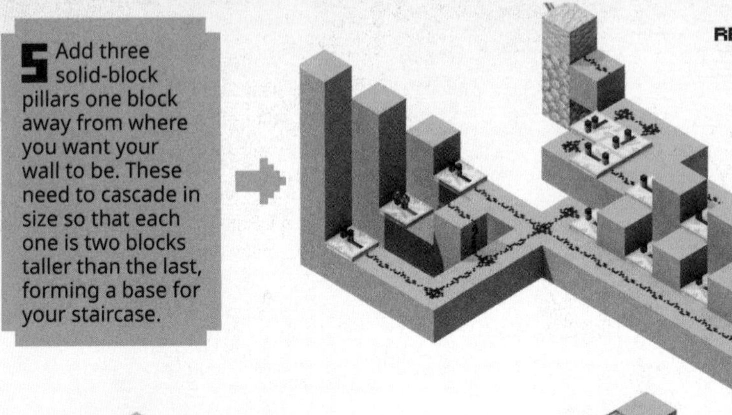

REVERSE VIEW

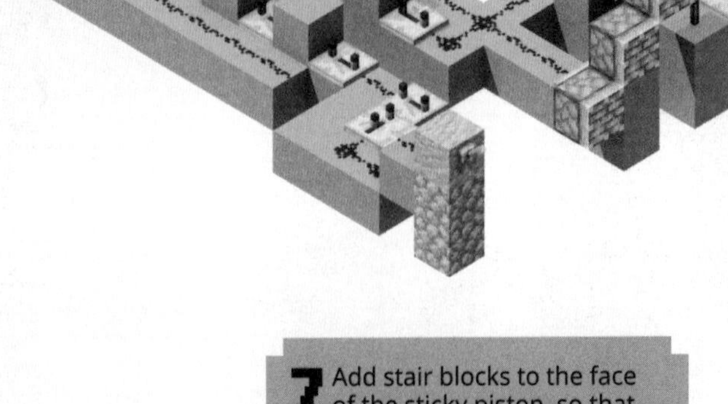

6 Add a sticky piston to the top of each pillar, facing into the base, and another on the left side of the top block of each pillar, facing the same way. On the middle and tallest pillars, replace the blocks with redstone torches as shown.

7 Add stair blocks to the face of the sticky piston, so that they're perpendicular to the wall and make a staircase. If you placed the sticky pistons correctly, you should be able to walk up the staircase already.

The stair blocks will be visible in your wall when it's built, so you can pick stairs that will blend in if you want it to look inconspicuous.

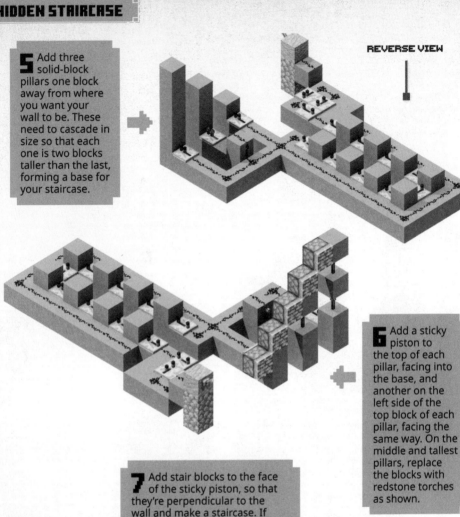

8 Go back to the original lever tower you built in step 2. This will become part of the inside wall of your base, so use the same blocks so it all matches. This wall will also contain the hidden staircase

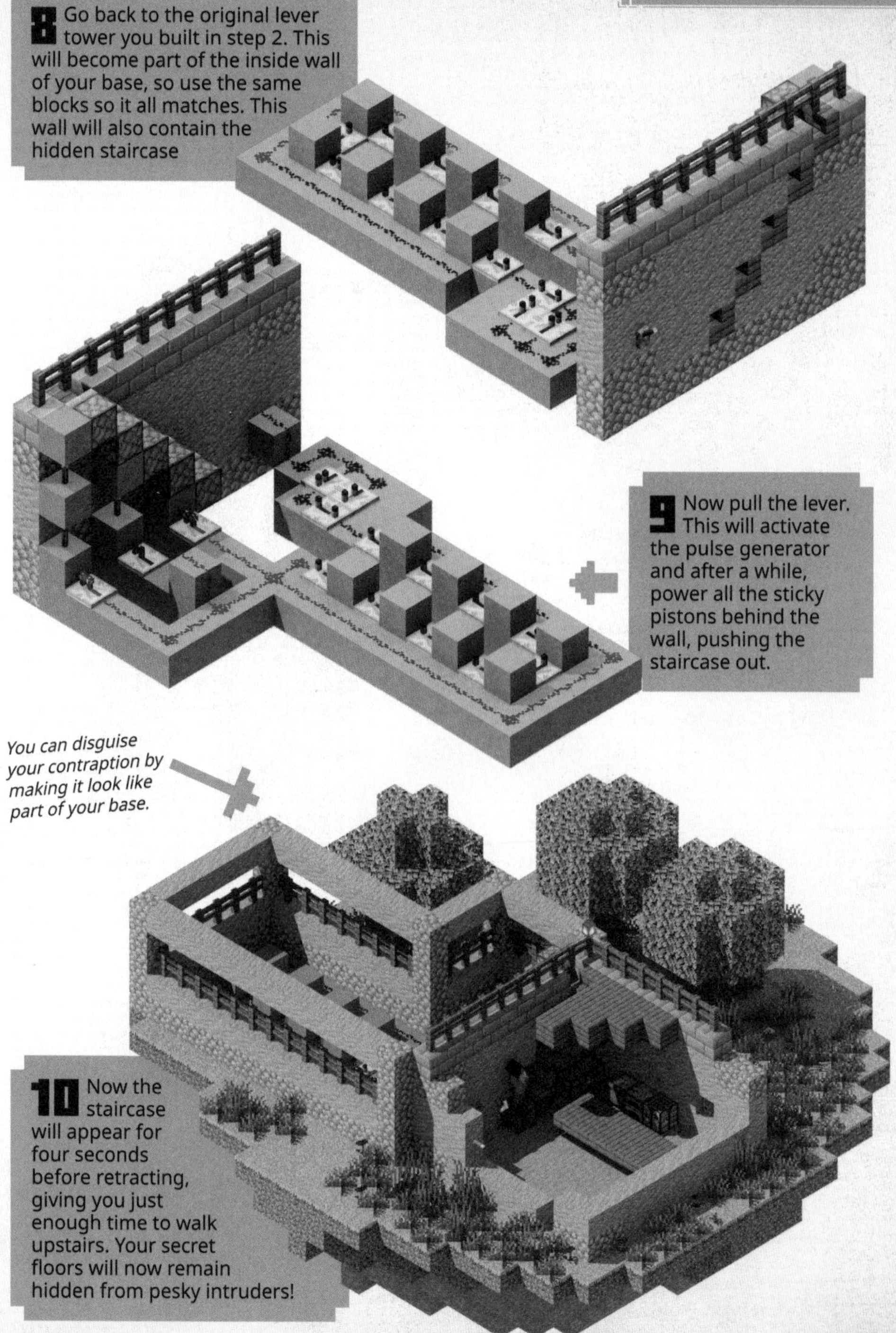

9 Now pull the lever. This will activate the pulse generator and after a while, power all the sticky pistons behind the wall, pushing the staircase out.

You can disguise your contraption by making it look like part of your base.

10 Now the staircase will appear for four seconds before retracting, giving you just enough time to walk upstairs. Your secret floors will now remain hidden from pesky intruders!

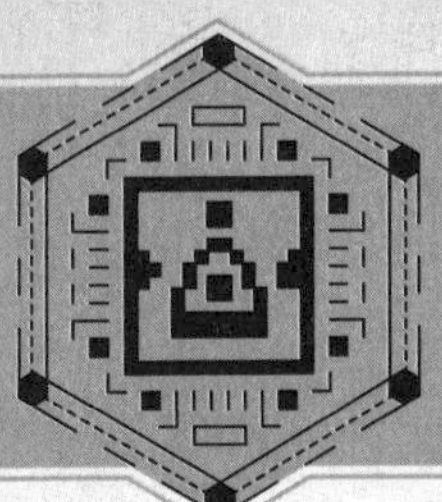

CLOCK CIRCUITS

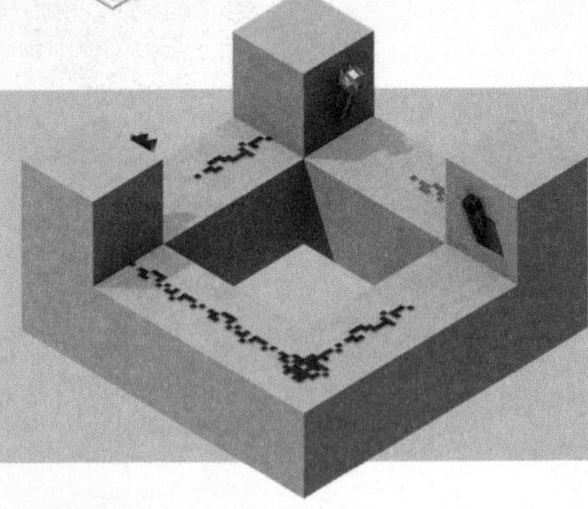

TORCH CLOCK

The easiest clock circuit uses redstone torches attached to solid blocks and linked with redstone dust. Each of these torch block combos is a NOT gate, which turns off when it receives a signal from behind. You need an odd number of torches in a torch clock, otherwise the signal will become stable.

REPEATER CLOCK

You can make a much faster clock circuit using repeaters. First you'll need 2 repeaters side-by-side, facing in opposite directions, then add redstone dust in front and behind each one. This is the clock, but you'll need a temporary power source to activate it. Place a redstone torch beside the dust and destroy it to begin the clock. You want to do this quickly – if the signal lasts for longer than 1, it won't loop.

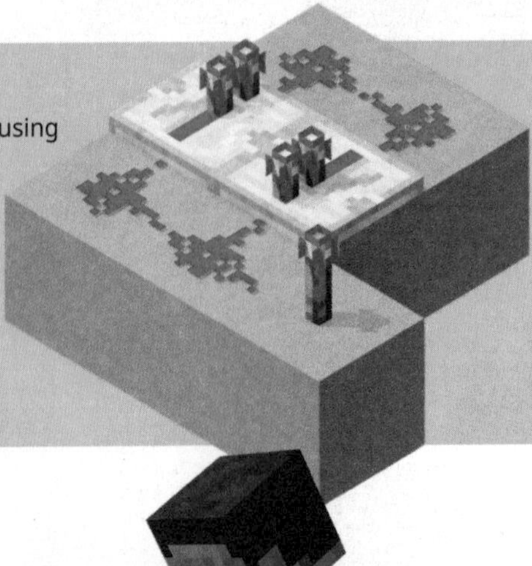

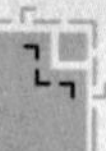

Rather than using a single pulse to activate your redstone contraption, you may need to make a regular signal. Clock circuits are basically loops of redstone signals that can repeatedly activate redstone components. Let's have a look at a few different ways we can make them.

TORCH-REPEATER CLOCK

Combining torches and repeaters gives you a happy medium between the two previous examples. They have a torch inverter NOT gate, so there's no chance of overpowering the repeaters, and it's capable of a 3-tick loop rather than the 5 of a torch clock. To make one, simply place repeaters side-by-side and in opposite directions, then place a solid block in front of one of them, with a torch facing out the side to power behind the second repeater. Add three redstone dusts on the other side of the repeaters and there you have it!

HOPPER CLOCK

The most compact clock circuit is created with hoppers. Place two adjacent hoppers, with their output tubes facing each other, then drop an item in. Add a comparator facing away from one hopper. Like the repeater clock, it needs to be briefly activated by a power source, so add and destroy a torch beside a hopper. The item will be passed back and forth between the hoppers, and the comparator will output a signal regularly when it detects it in the hopper behind it.

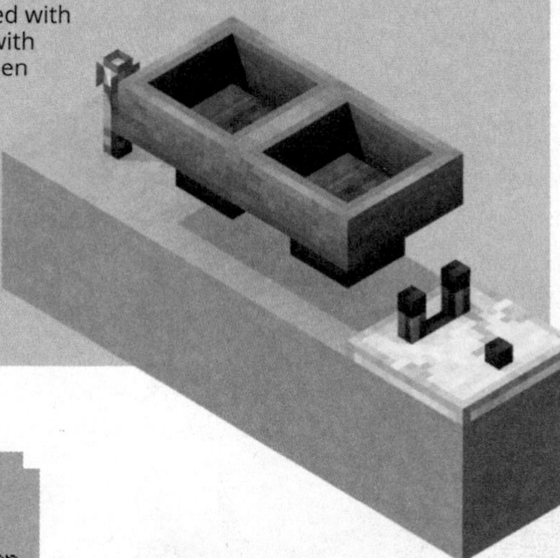

TOP TIP

Once a hopper clock is running, you can add a comparator beside the other hopper to create two alternating clocks from the same source.

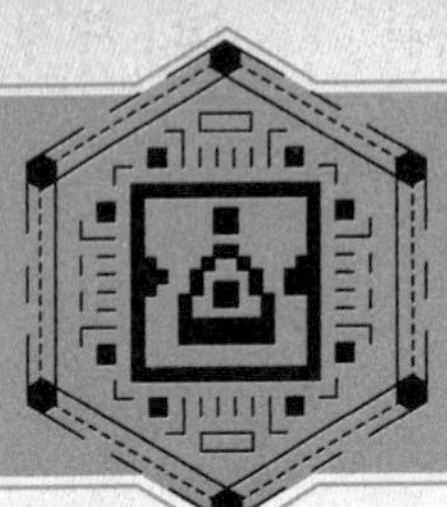

ARTILLERY ROW

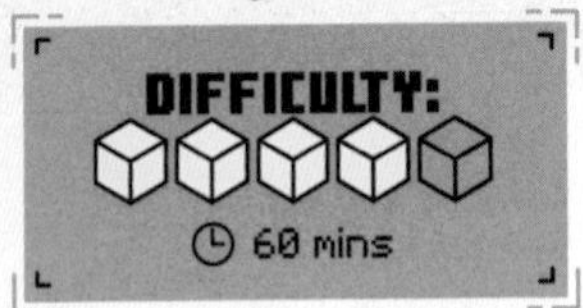

MAIN BLOCKS

FRONT

SIDE

TOP

Clock circuits are great for repeatedly activating redstone mechanisms, particularly weaponised ones. This row of arrow cannons will receive regular redstone signals and launch an arrow every time they receive the signal. This is a great way to keep invaders at bay.

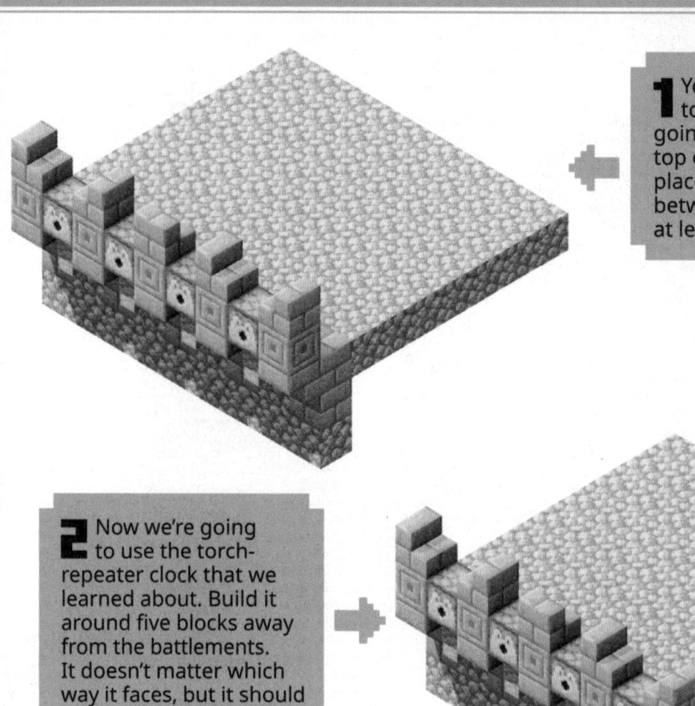

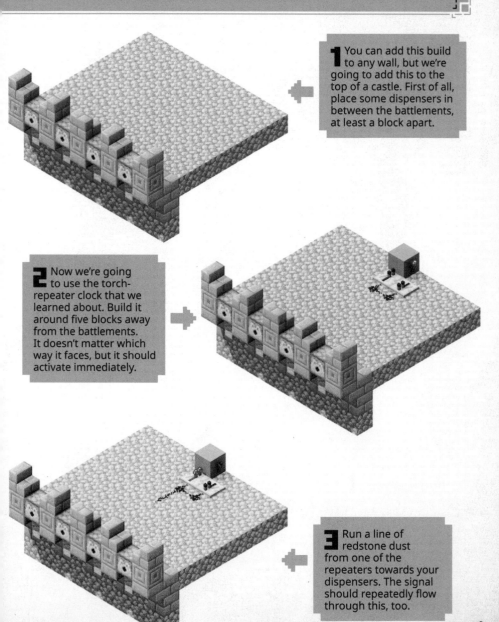

1 You can add this build to any wall, but we're going to add this to the top of a castle. First of all, place some dispensers in between the battlements, at least a block apart.

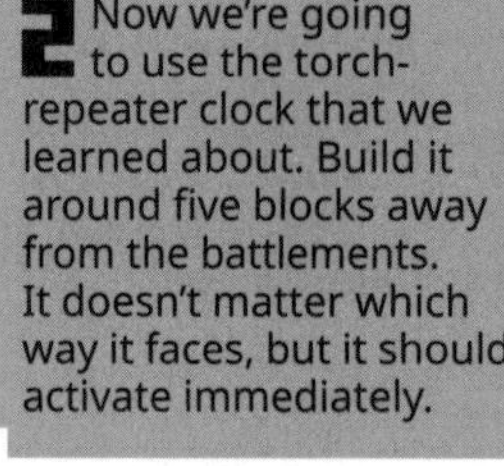

2 Now we're going to use the torch-repeater clock that we learned about. Build it around five blocks away from the battlements. It doesn't matter which way it faces, but it should activate immediately.

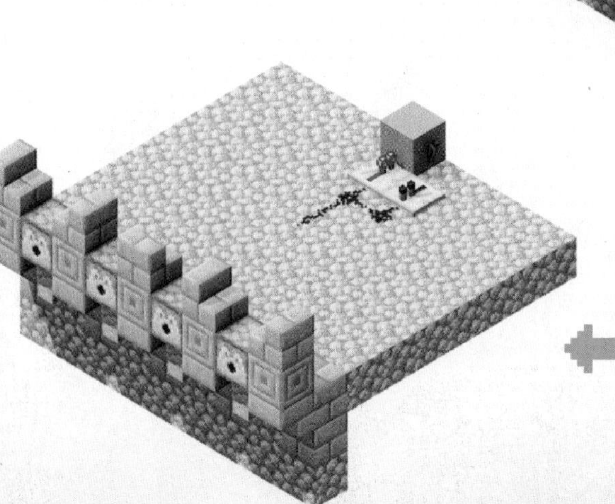

3 Run a line of redstone dust from one of the repeaters towards your dispensers. The signal should repeatedly flow through this, too.

4 Now we want to add a breaker between the circuit and the dispensers, otherwise you'll run out of arrows before invaders get anywhere near. Add a torch inverter NOT gate at the end of the redstone dust and place a lever on the top of it.

TOP VIEW

5 In front of the torch inverter, run more redstone and then branch it out so that redstone is going into each of the dispensers. The NOT gate should be stopping the signal reaching the dispensers at the moment. If not, then flick the lever.

6 Fill the dispensers with arrows. You should add as many stacks of 64 arrows as you can, so that you can avoid refilling too often.

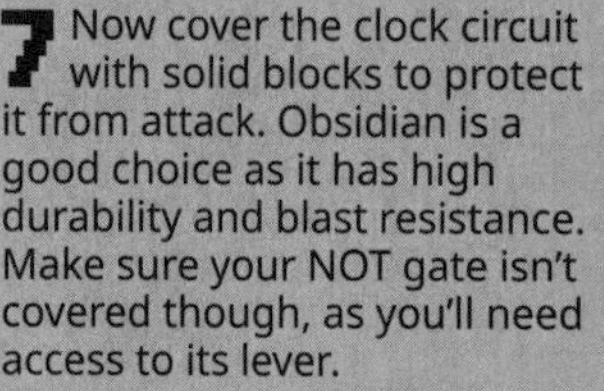

7 Now cover the clock circuit with solid blocks to protect it from attack. Obsidian is a good choice as it has high durability and blast resistance. Make sure your NOT gate isn't covered though, as you'll need access to its lever.

8 Pull the lever on the NOT gate to let the signal flow through the torch inverter and activate the dispensers. The arrows should start flying simultaneously from all the dispensers.

9 The clock circuit will be constantly running, but you can use that lever to enable the dispensers to receive the signal whenever attackers appear within range. If you want to conceal your weapon, you can also link the clock circuits to fence gates, so that they are hidden when not in use.

REDSTONE HACKS

PRECISE SIGNAL STRENGTH

Some builds will need a redstone signal that only travels a certain distance, but most power sources are all or nothing. Using a combination of a sticky piston, a comparator and a storage block, you can create a power source of exact strength by filling the storage item up to the correct degree. Then you can use a button to extend the storage item to the comparator and produce that perfect signal.

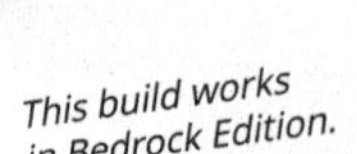

This build works in Bedrock Edition.

MISDIRECTION

If you want to stop your redstone signal powering blocks that it passes by as it travels vertically, you can place items to redirect the signal. Normally your wire will continue on past the irrelevant block, but, if it's at the end of a circuit for example, you can place a target block beyond the block you want to skip to then direct the redstone away. The target block attracts the redstone because it's a redstone block, but has no function when powered.

This build works in Java Edition.

Now you've learnt the basic circuits, you're on the path to becoming an engineering legend. To cement your place in the redstone hall of fame, here are some expert tips to help you on your way before we look at the final builds.

WIRELESS USAGE

Redstone without wires is rare but not impossible. The simplest example is skulk sensors, which emit redstone signals when activated by nearby vibrations. An alternative solution is to deploy two daylight detectors and comparing their signals. It's possible to use a block attached to a piston to block the daylight and pass a signal down without wires. There can't be any other blocks in the way, it has to be daytime, and it has to be clear weather – so it won't work all the time.

SUBSTITUTION

We've already looked at lots of different circuits, but get used to toying around with them to create useful equipment. One head-smackingly obvious way to create a clock circuit is by using a rail circuit, with intermittent powered rails and a detector rail, which will output a signal every time a minecart passes over it. It's not the most compact build, but it's probably the easiest.

TOP TIP

Swap power sources, manipulation blocks and outputs to see how you can extend and elaborate on your unique redstone builds.

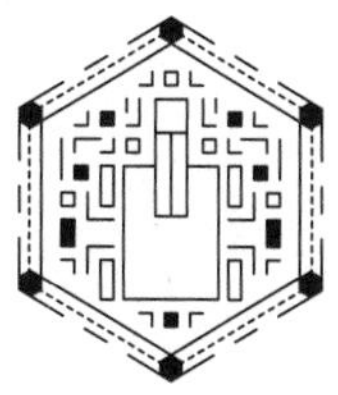

REDSTONE WORKSHOP

By now you'll have got a taste for what's possible with redstone, but that's just the beginning. This section will tie together various components, behaviours and circuits to create jaw-dropping contraptions that will help you mine, fend off invaders and keep your treasures safe.

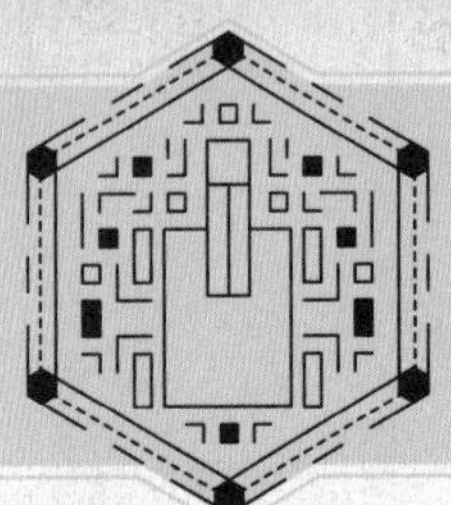

LAVA DROP TRAP

DIFFICULTY:

60 mins

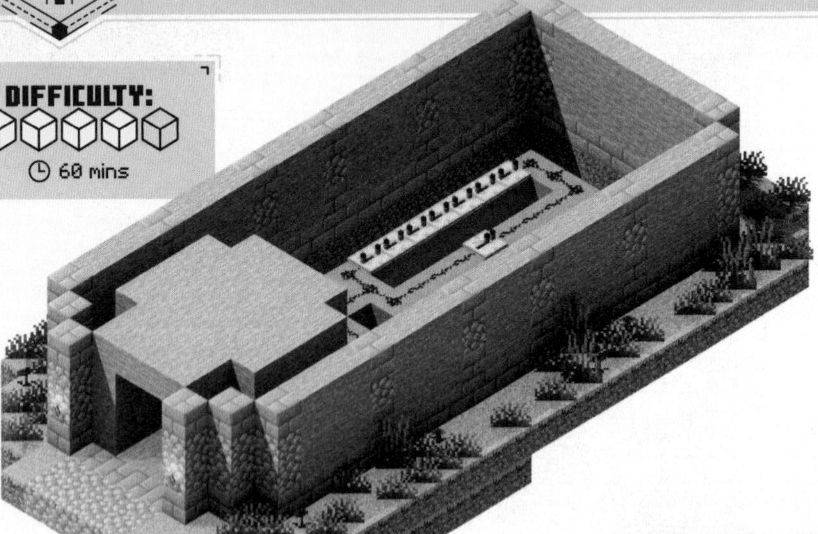

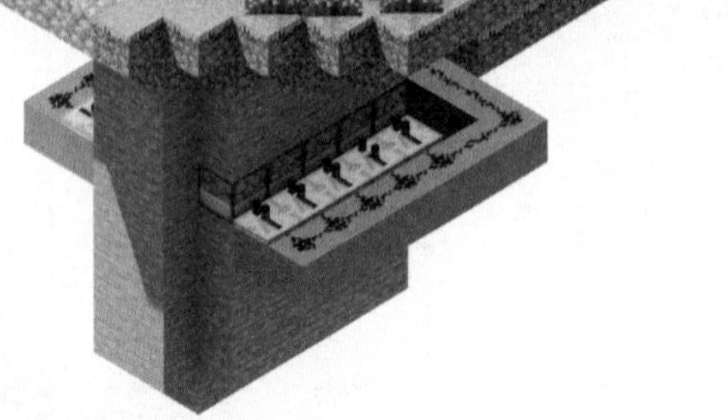

MAIN BLOCKS

FRONT

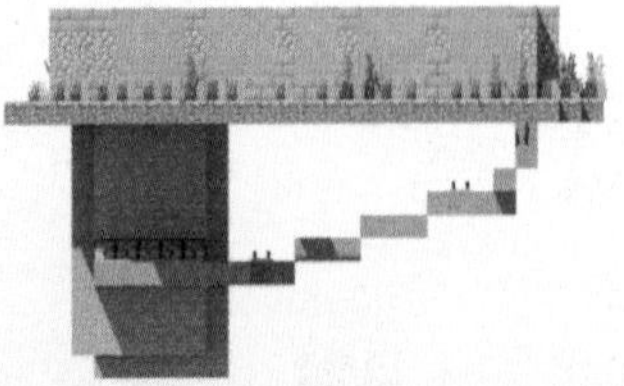

SIDE

TOP

If the lava doesn't get you, the drop will. This two-pronged trap attack uses a pulse circuit and vertical redstone to simultaneously open up the floor to a steep pitfall and release lava on top of the unsuspecting – and plummeting – thieves.

1 Dig a deep trench in the ground, at least 2x5 blocks wide and 10 blocks deep. Place 2 trapped chests on top of new solid blocks at one edge of the trench – the wall of the build will be behind the trapped chest.

2 Place two rows of sticky pistons in front of the trapped chest, so that they're facing each other.

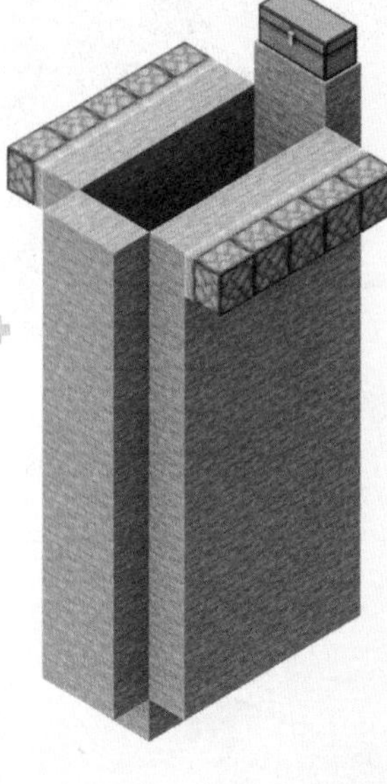

3 Place a solid block one space behind each of the sticky pistons and run redstone dust along the top. At the end of these new rows, add a block one space higher, two spaces along, so it's in line with the chest. Place a redstone torch on them. This should activate your pistons and create your pitfall floor.

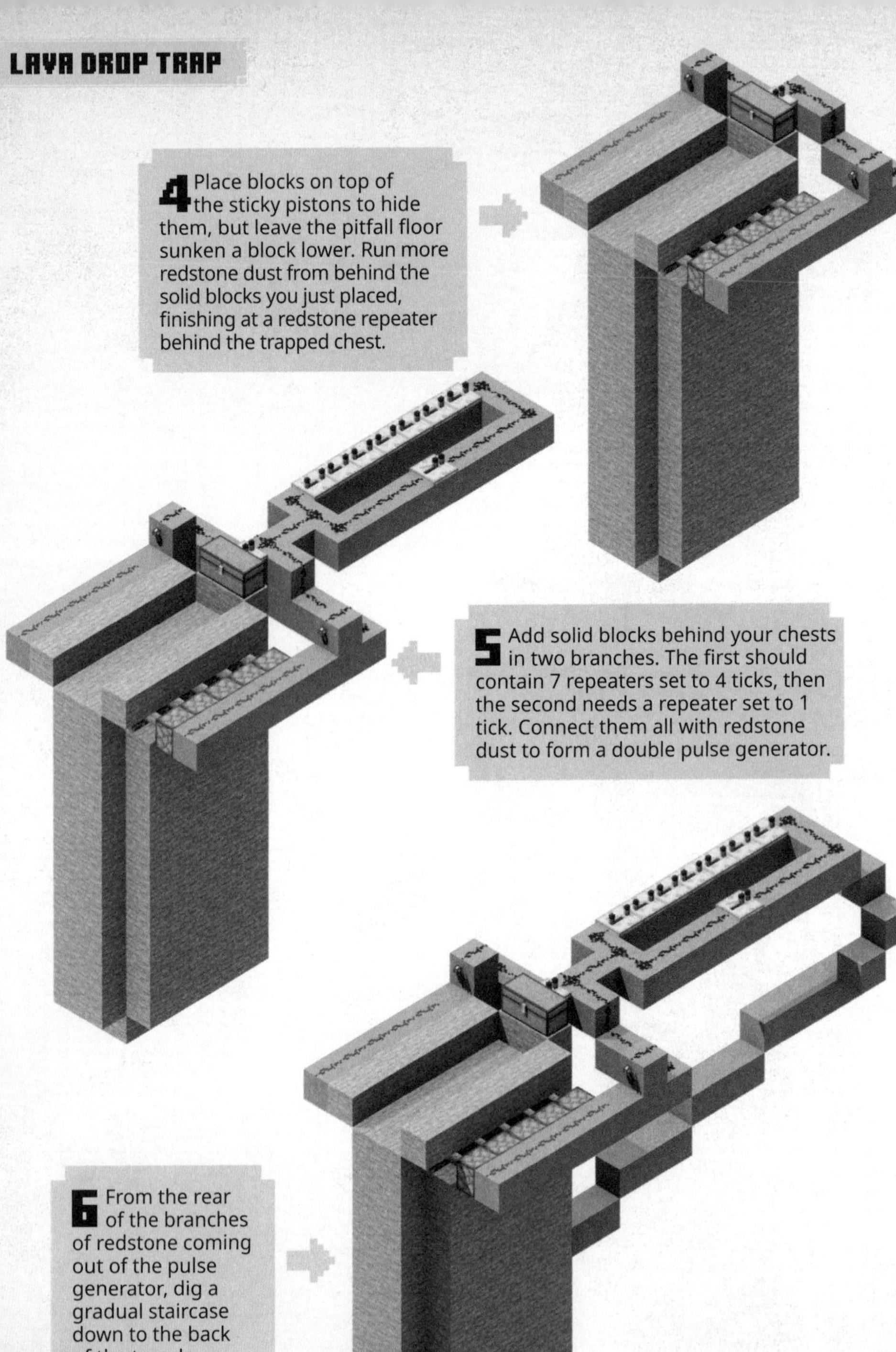

4 Place blocks on top of the sticky pistons to hide them, but leave the pitfall floor sunken a block lower. Run more redstone dust from behind the solid blocks you just placed, finishing at a redstone repeater behind the trapped chest.

5 Add solid blocks behind your chests in two branches. The first should contain 7 repeaters set to 4 ticks, then the second needs a repeater set to 1 tick. Connect them all with redstone dust to form a double pulse generator.

6 From the rear of the branches of redstone coming out of the pulse generator, dig a gradual staircase down to the back of the trench.

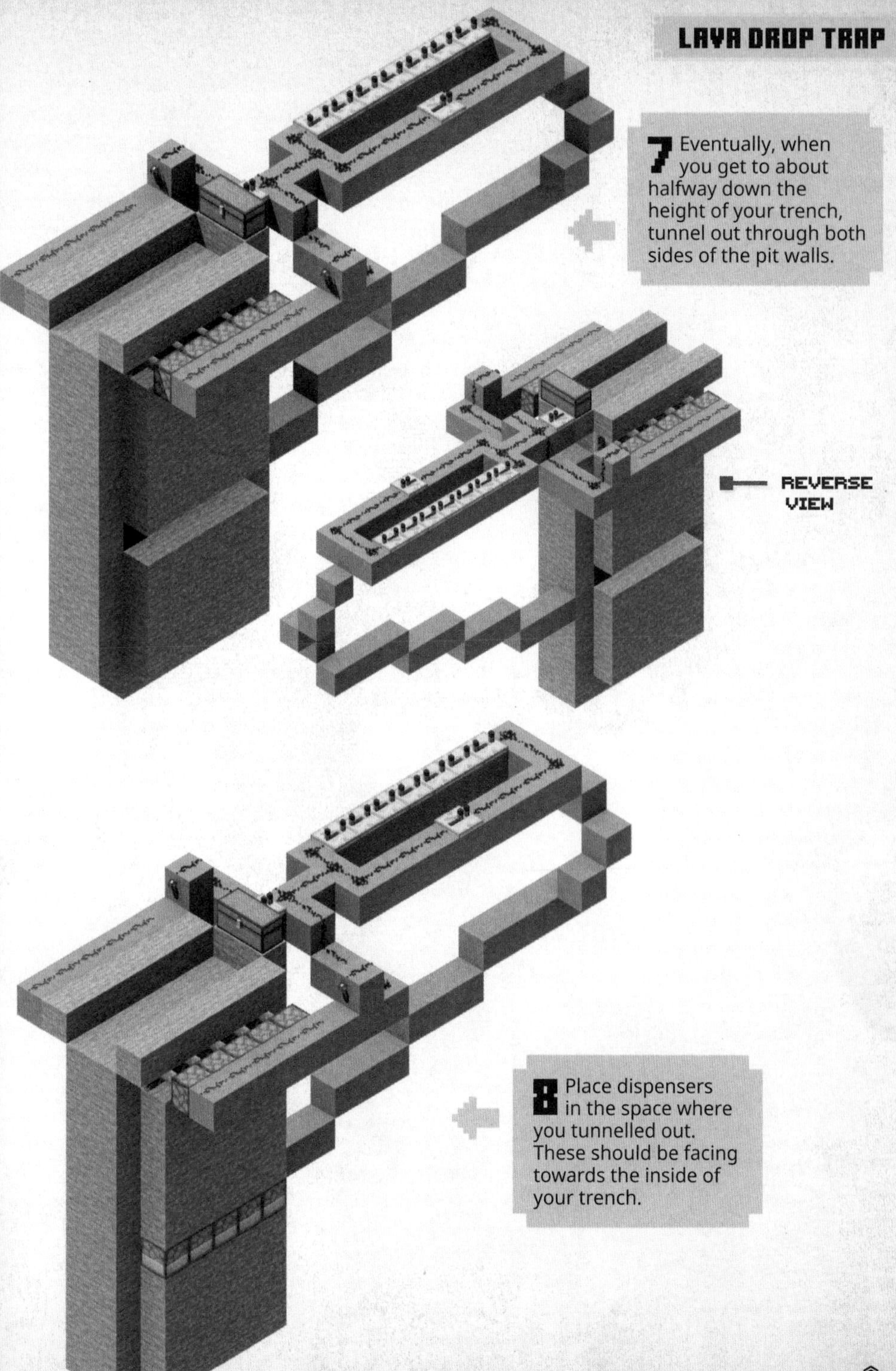

7 Eventually, when you get to about halfway down the height of your trench, tunnel out through both sides of the pit walls.

8 Place dispensers in the space where you tunnelled out. These should be facing towards the inside of your trench.

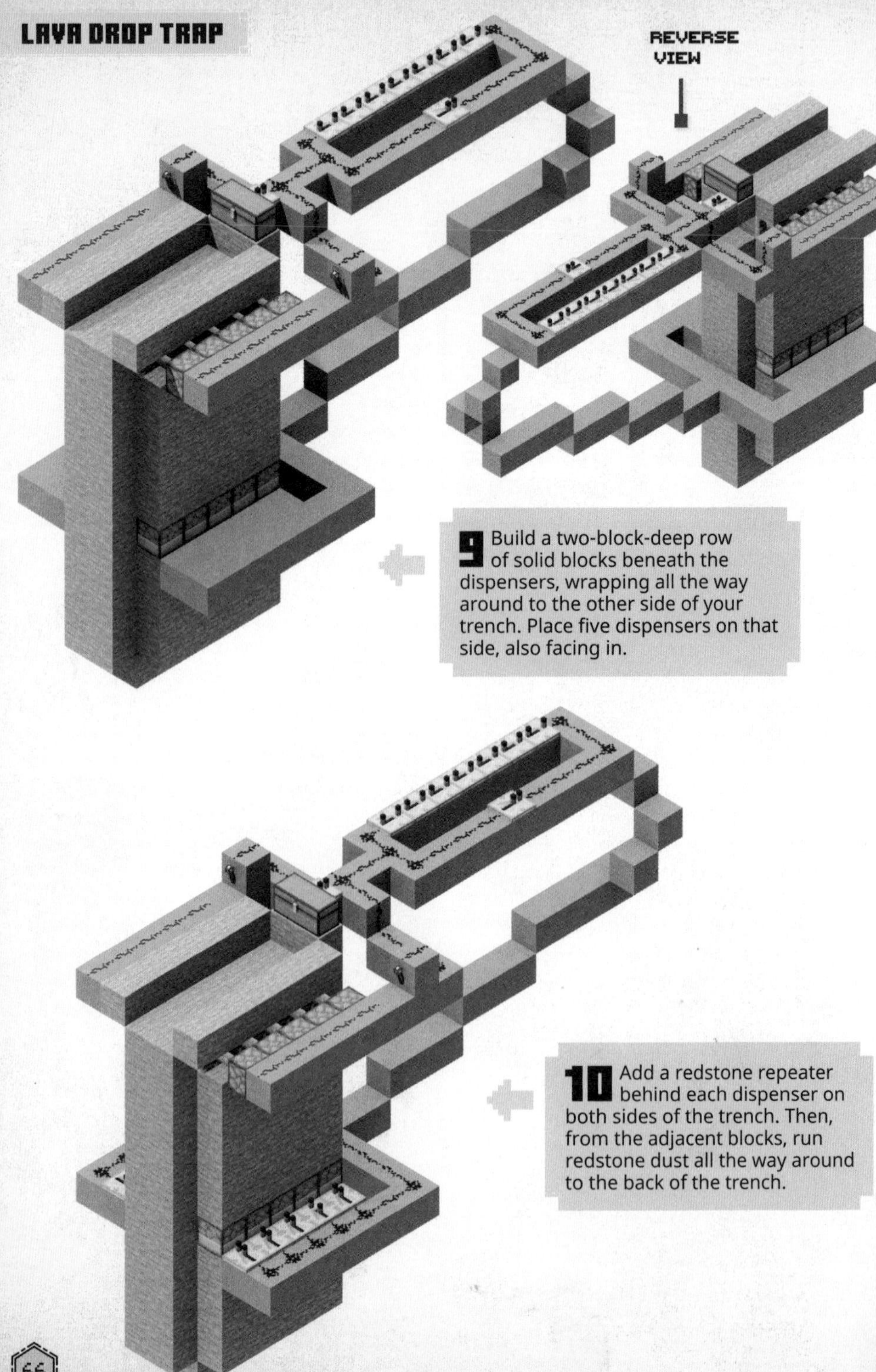

9 Build a two-block-deep row of solid blocks beneath the dispensers, wrapping all the way around to the other side of your trench. Place five dispensers on that side, also facing in.

10 Add a redstone repeater behind each dispenser on both sides of the trench. Then, from the adjacent blocks, run redstone dust all the way around to the back of the trench.

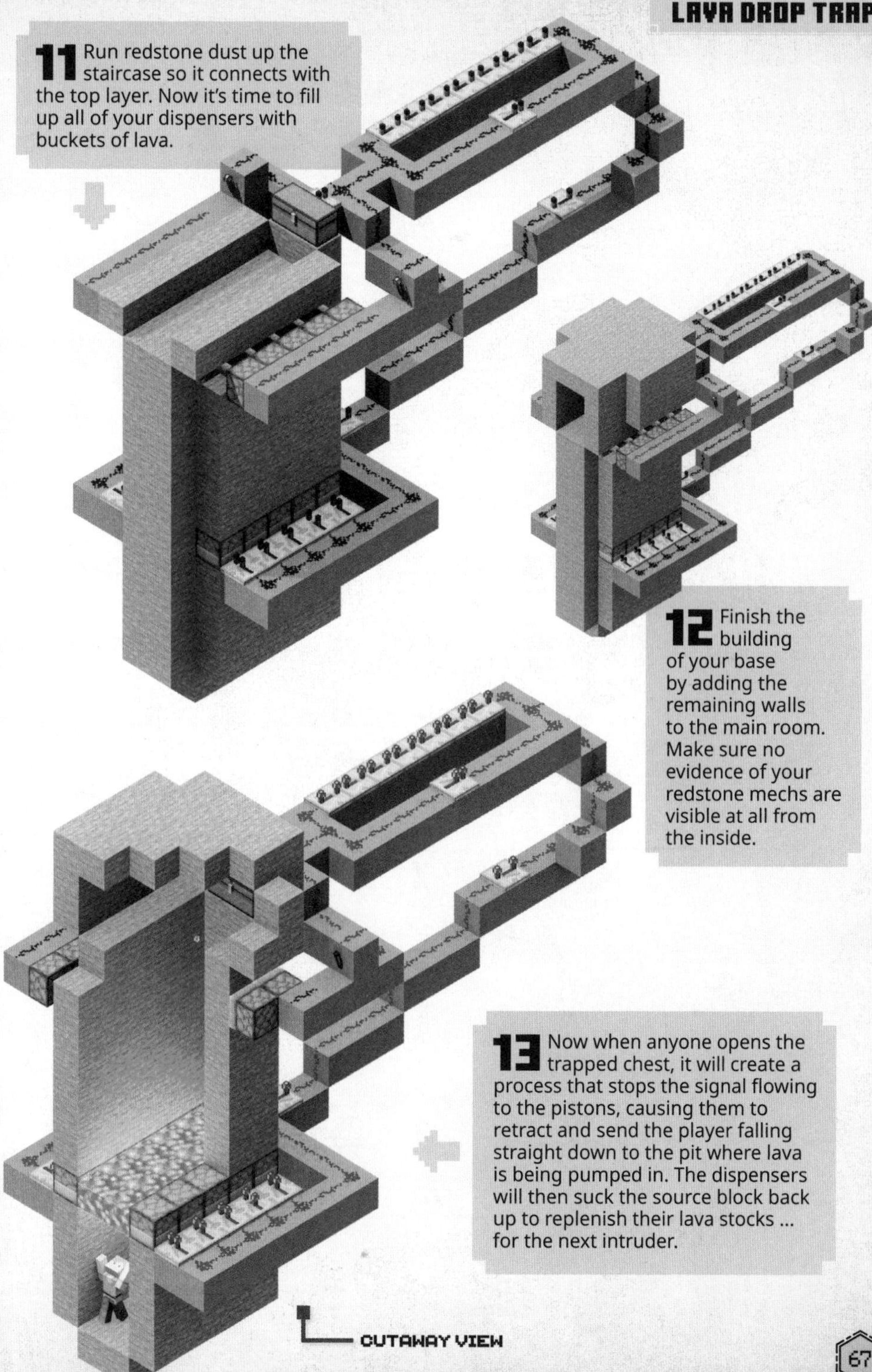

11 Run redstone dust up the staircase so it connects with the top layer. Now it's time to fill up all of your dispensers with buckets of lava.

12 Finish the building of your base by adding the remaining walls to the main room. Make sure no evidence of your redstone mechs are visible at all from the inside.

13 Now when anyone opens the trapped chest, it will create a process that stops the signal flowing to the pistons, causing them to retract and send the player falling straight down to the pit where lava is being pumped in. The dispensers will then suck the source block back up to replenish their lava stocks ... for the next intruder.

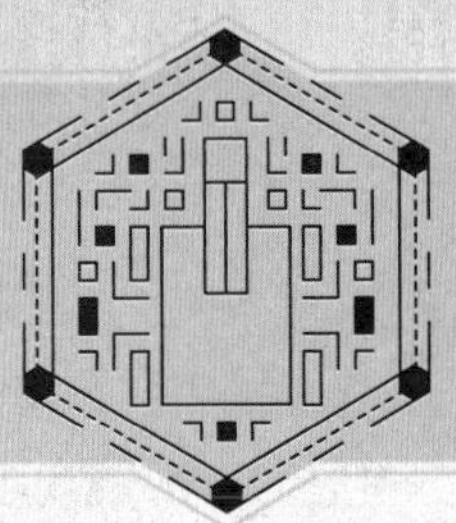

ALTERNATIVE DROP TRAPS

'RANDOM' DROP

Picture this – someone raids your base and uses the trapped chest, but nothing happens. So they move in and use it as their own HQ for a while, continuing to use the chest. Then one time they use it, they suddenly drop into a trap. If you add a pulse divider behind the trapped chest before it reaches the rest of the mechanism, it will only activate on the sixth opening. It's a long play, but it could be worth the wait.

Experiment with all the redstone blocks you've come across in this book. How will your trap work?

NOT A DROP TO DRINK

Lava's all well and good, but water can be just as deadly if used correctly. Instead of having lava flood the trench, fill it with water so it's flush with the blocks that the pistons are stuck to, so when it closes up, intruders will become stuck underwater instead of being torched! If you don't disable the lava drop element, it will create blocks of obsidian that will make it even harder for trapped intruders to mine their way to freedom.

Now you've finished off your lava drop trap, it's time to think how you can make it even better. Part of the fun of redstone is playing about to see how you can change and improve parts. This spread shows a few ways you can take the build and adapt it to fit your needs.

FIGHT FOR FREEDOM

What could be more of a shock for an unwelcome intruder than plummeting into an unexpected fight pit? This trap will drop players into a shallow pool in the middle of a room with mob spawners! From the moment they splash down, it will be one fast-paced battle to try to escape unharmed.

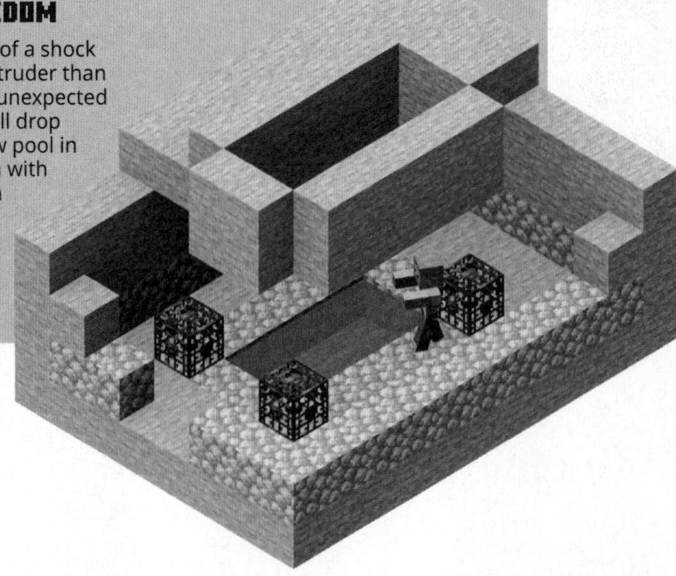

GAME TIME

Maybe you want to toy with the intruders rather than ruthlessly injure them. If you've got the time and inclination, you can add clock circuits behind each of the pitfall pistons to make them randomly open and close. Then sit back and watch the invaders hop around to try to avoid falling to their doom.

Putting the time into your traps can make them unpredictable and difficult to beat!

THEN AND NOW WITH: JIGARBOV

THEN

'I still have my very first redstone usage, from way back in Alpha v1.1.2_01. I was tired of running into my house and closing the door behind me to protect myself from creepers, so I worked out how to make it close automatically using this little contraption ... This first build just shows how little I knew about redstone at the start. Why was there even redstone dust between the button and the door? I thought it was necessary to connect the two, but how wrong I was.'

'Not long after this, I moved into my first "real" redstone project, an intercontinental train station! Knowing nothing about chunks or how they worked, I required a couple of midway stations because depending on the direction of the minecart, the boosters had to be orientated a certain way ... What even are boosters?'

'Boosters were how we used to give minecarts more speed because we didn't have powered rails back then. When two minecarts moved on a track together, they would both generate more speed due to a collision glitch ... The problem with boosters is that they were directional, so it mattered which way I was going on the rail! If I were to make this now, I would simply replace this whole thing with a couple of powered rails. How things have changed.'

It's amazing how much your skills can improve once you dive head first into redstone. Jigarbov is back to demonstrate just how much better you can get with hard work and dedication. Let's take a look at his first and latest redstone builds to see how he's progressed.

NOW

'A long time after those little experiments in Survival, I started map making. That is the art of creating a world for players to explore and deliver a story, or adventure, or puzzles and minigames. While most people use command blocks for that now, redstone is still often used at the core. A few friends and I even made an entire adventure map in Survival mode using nothing but redstone! We released a full adventure map called "Perhaps, The Last" and my quest involved going into an ocean monument and completing a bunch of puzzles.'

'It starts off as a simple timing puzzle where the player must move an egg through the tube and get it to the other side. We used hidden redstone circuits and slime blocks on pistons to bounce the eggs around and get it to the end. The complexity ramps up in the second part where the player must move the egg through a more complex array of tubes by manipulating a series of pistons to change the water flow. It culminates in a redstone repeater locking challenge that will make the minecart move all the way to the end of the track, fill the items into the hoppers and complete the challenge.'

'Many of the puzzles here actually teach very foundational redstone mechanics. Redstone is not limited to just making your Survival world better, or making a huge walking robot, you can also use it to tell a story and engage your friends and others in the creation of puzzles and a whole host of wonderful things.'

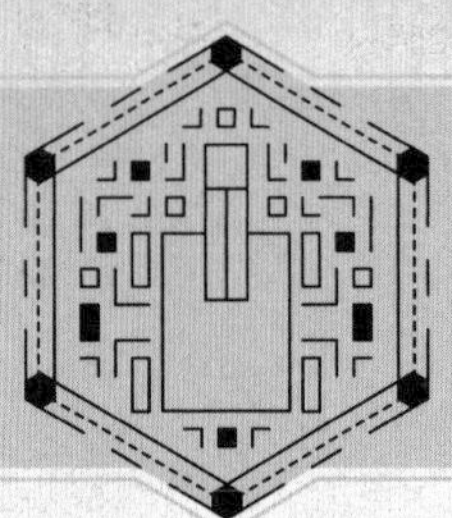

RAIL ENTRANCE LOCK

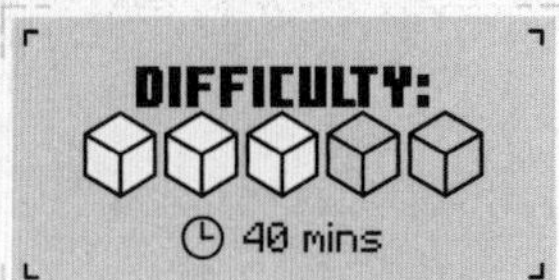

MAIN BLOCKS

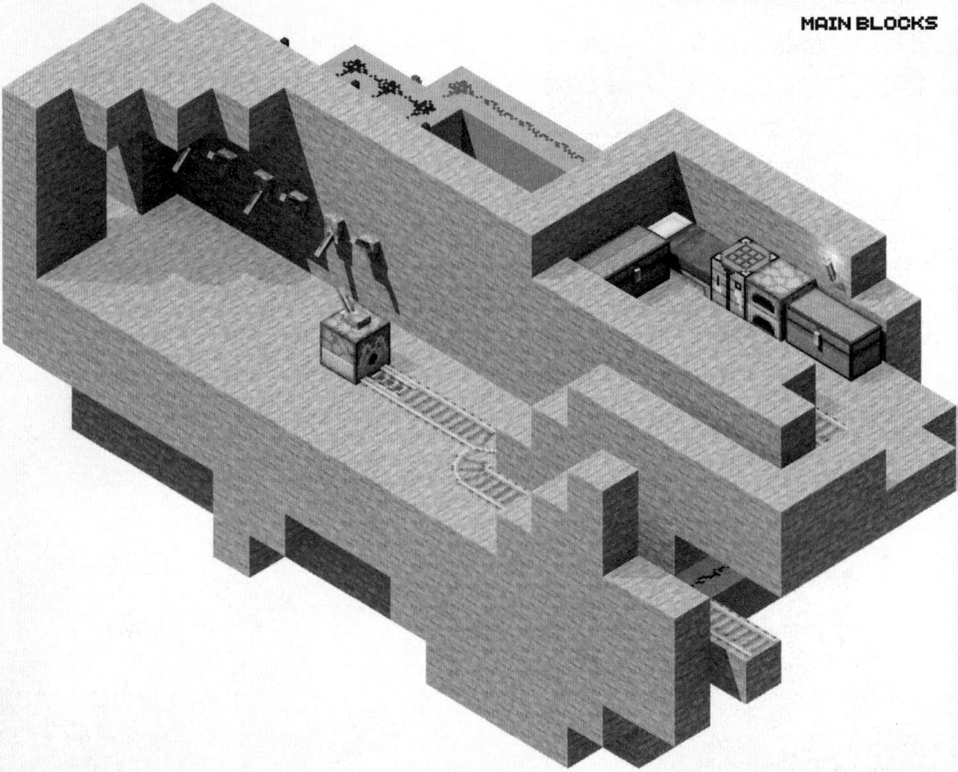

FRONT

SIDE

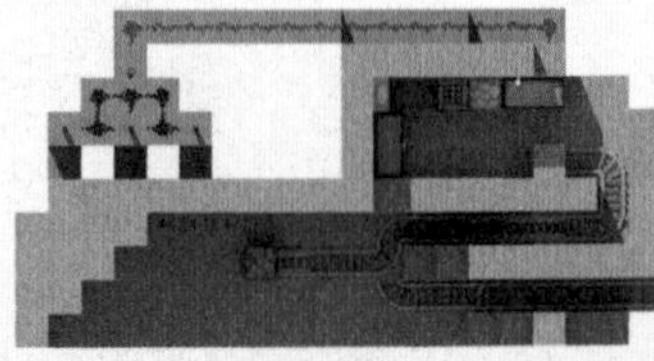

TOP

Another way to keep your base safe is by being sneaky. The rail entrance lock makes it look like you can just hop into a minecart and enter the base, but the combination lock wall makes it so only those in the know will make it inside – anyone else will meet a sheer drop off a cliff.

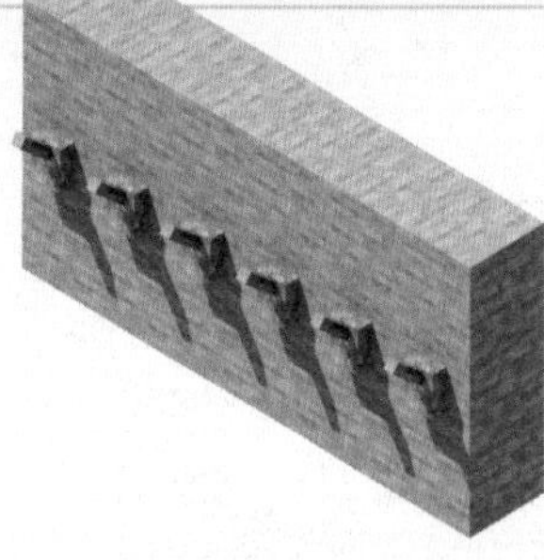

1 Build a 3x6 wall outside of your base using solid blocks. Place levers along the middle row of blocks to create the start of the combination lock.

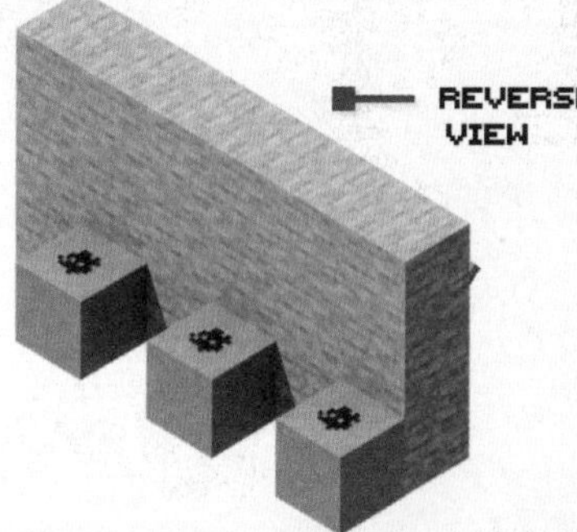

2 Choose three of the levers to form your secret entry code. Place a block behind these 3 and place redstone dust on top of each of them.

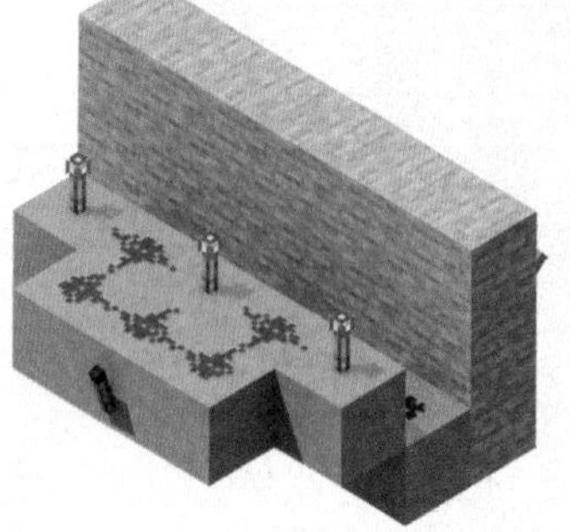

3 Behind that redstone, build a raised three-input AND gate (as seen on page 41). Place solid blocks to make the platform, add redstone torches on the blocks directly behind the redstone you just placed, then cover the remaining blocks with redstone dust. Place a redstone torch in the middle on the back of the platform.

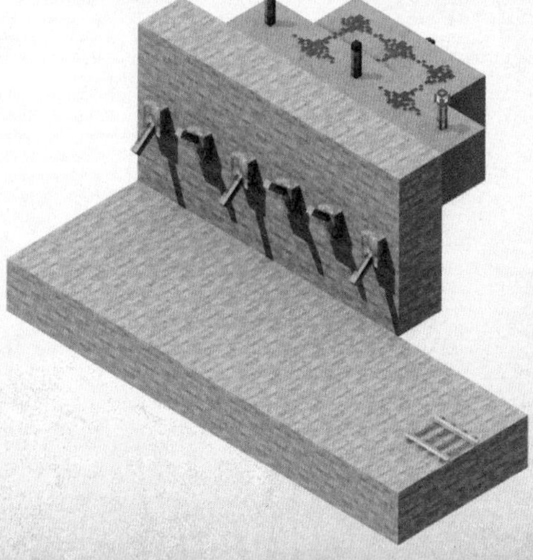

4 Do a quick test by activating the levers to make sure that the AND gate is set up correctly and leaves just one torch turned on behind the wall. Then decide where to start the fork of your railway.

RAIL ENTRANCE LOCK

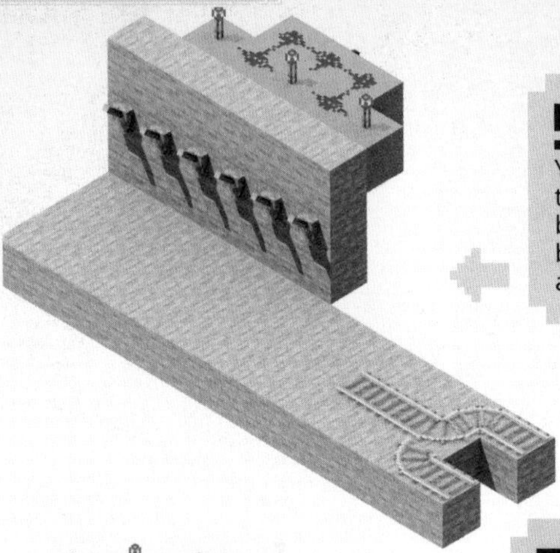

5 Continue your railway and make it branch out in two directions. You'll see the junction curve added to the rail between the start of the branches. You'll need a block gap between the branching paths, so dig a trench between them.

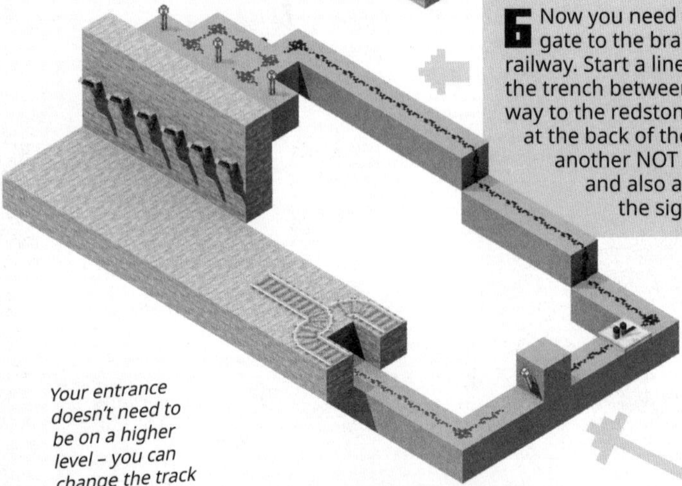

6 Now you need to connect the AND gate to the branching part of your railway. Start a line of redstone dust in the trench between the branches, all the way to the redstone torch you placed at the back of the AND gate. There's another NOT gate along the way, and also a repeater to increase the signal strength.

Your entrance doesn't need to be on a higher level – you can change the track to better suit your own base design.

If you're playing in Bedrock Edition, you need to remove this NOT gate.

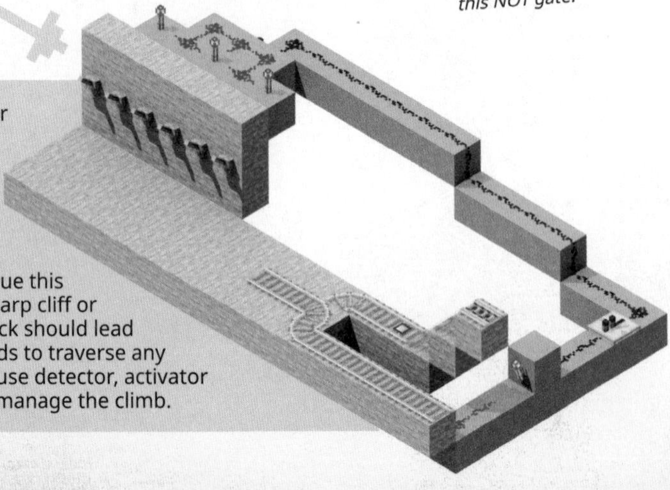

7 Now continue your branches away from the junction. With the levers all deactivated, the junction will divert your railway track to the trap route. Continue this doomed route to a sharp cliff or lava pit. The other track should lead to your base. If it needs to traverse any ramps, make sure to use detector, activator and powered rails to manage the climb.

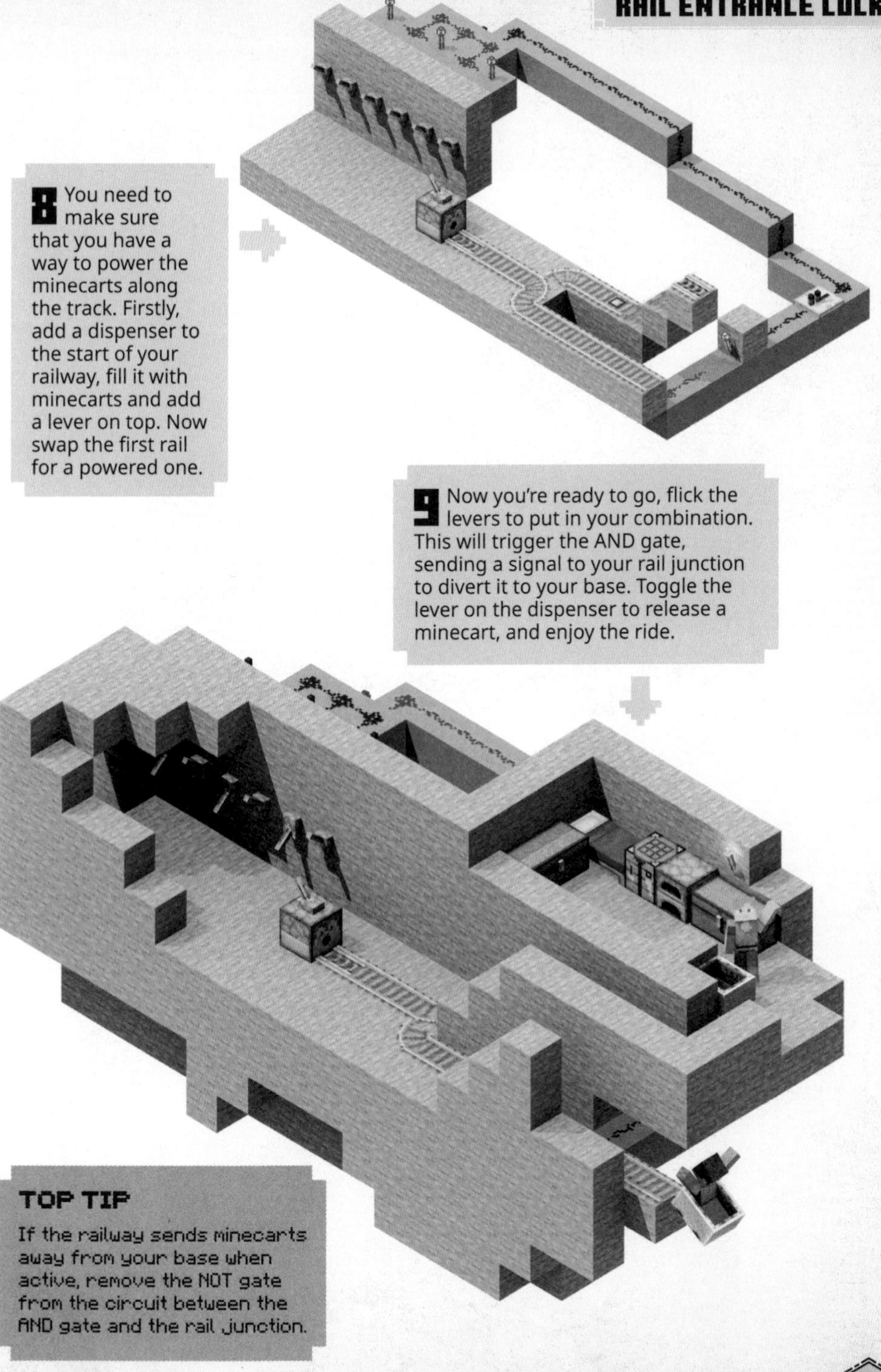

8 You need to make sure that you have a way to power the minecarts along the track. Firstly, add a dispenser to the start of your railway, fill it with minecarts and add a lever on top. Now swap the first rail for a powered one.

9 Now you're ready to go, flick the levers to put in your combination. This will trigger the AND gate, sending a signal to your rail junction to divert it to your base. Toggle the lever on the dispenser to release a minecart, and enjoy the ride.

TOP TIP

If the railway sends minecarts away from your base when active, remove the NOT gate from the circuit between the AND gate and the rail junction.

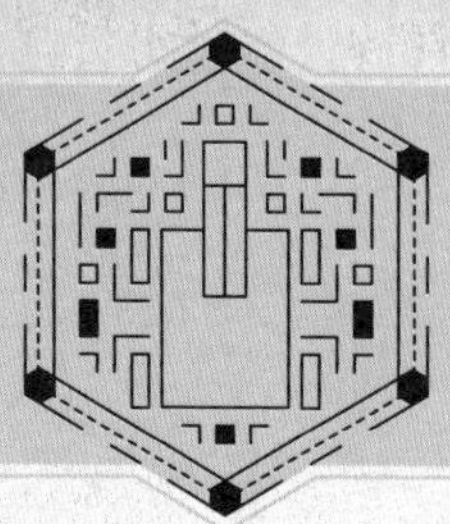

ALTERNATIVE ENTRANCE LOCKS

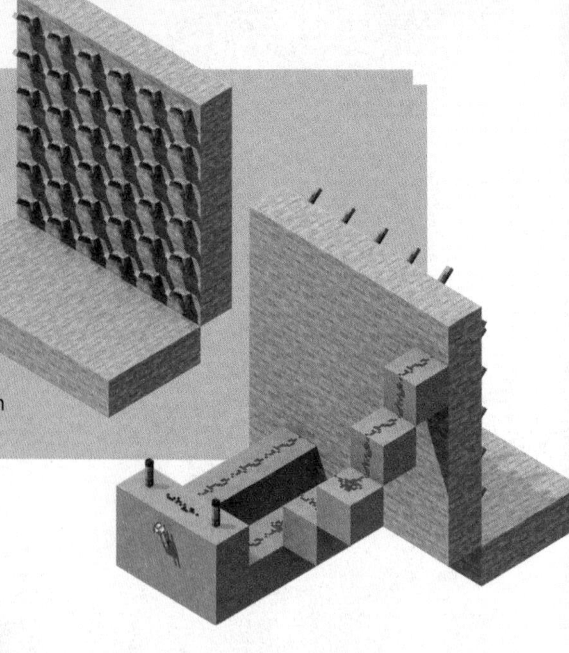

MAX SECURITY

With just six levers on the wall, there's a chance that unwelcome visitors may be able to guess which levers to pull. Put an end to any chances of that happening by building a bigger wall with lots more levers. You can use redstone staircases to get a redstone signal down from the higher levels. As long as you still have three inputs from somewhere, the circuit will work.

THE END?

Letting an invader's minecart fly off a cliff has a certain poetic justice to it, but if you really want to make things hard, build an end portal for them to fall into. They won't even be in the same dimension as you anymore and, even if they pop back through the portal, they'll still have to climb back up the cliff and try again.

Another build, another way to toy with invaders that are trying to get their hands on your hard-earned treasure – but the fun doesn't stop there. Have a look at these twists on the rail entrance lock formula to make things more secure, more exciting or even more punishing.

You can also be a little bit more generous with your booby-trapped track. Use combinations of detector rails and activated rails to give them a high-speed route away from your base without sending them off a cliff. Just make sure the end point is far enough away that they won't be back to bother you for a few days ...

The more twists, turns and ramps you add, the more likely you are to confuse invaders.

OFF THE RAILS

There's a chance that some invaders will just walk along the tracks instead of hopping in a minecart – the bunch of spoilsports – so if you want a solid lock on your base, you could just link the combination lock to an iron door or piston door mechanism. It's not as fun or theatrical, but it doesn't leave any chinks in your base's armour.

TOP TIP

Make sure you have lots of steep drops or powered rails in long routes so that your minecarts reach their destination.

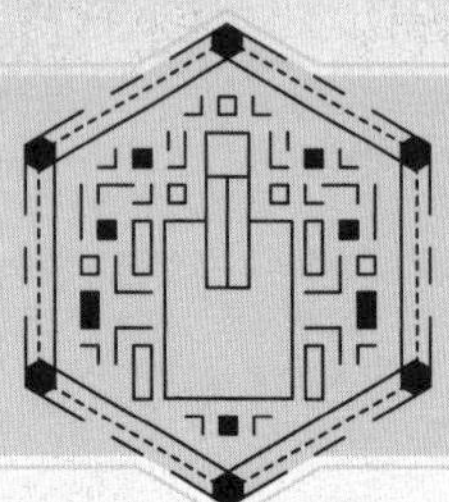

LECTERN SELECTOR

DIFFICULTY:

90 mins

MAIN BLOCKS

FRONT

SIDE

TOP

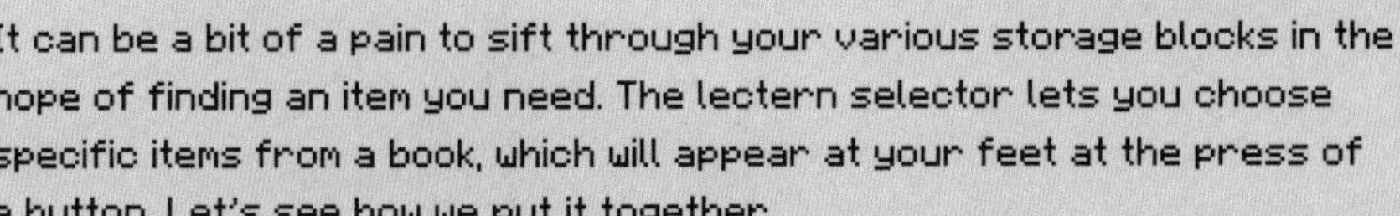

It can be a bit of a pain to sift through your various storage blocks in the hope of finding an item you need. The lectern selector lets you choose specific items from a book, which will appear at your feet at the press of a button. Let's see how we put it together.

1 Place a lectern in a clear space and put a book on top of it. The page number of the book corresponds to the strength of the signal it produces.

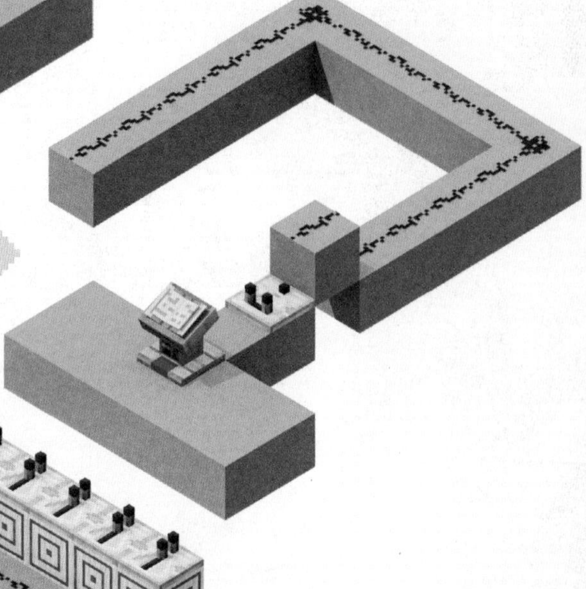

2 Place 2 solid blocks behind the lectern with a comparator on the second block. Behind the comparator, add a solid block with redstone dust on top. Run a line of solid blocks and redstone dust for 15 blocks behind in a horseshoe formation.

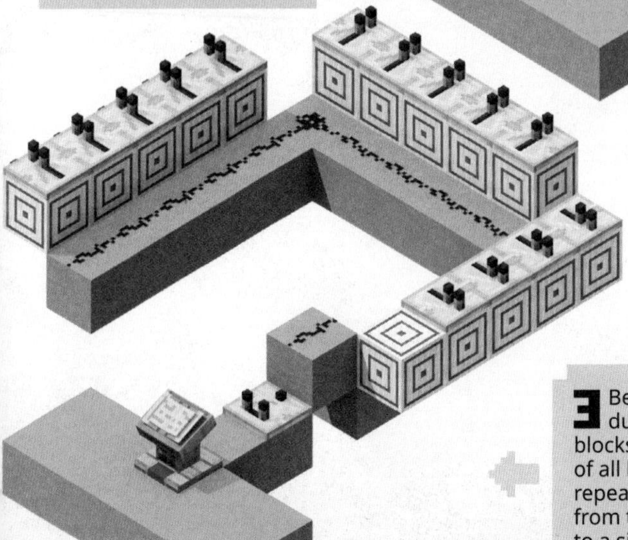

3 Beside that line of redstone dust, add rows of target blocks with repeaters on top of all but the first one. The repeaters should be facing away from the redstone dust and set to a single tick.

LECTERN SELECTOR

4 Put a redstone torch on the outside face of each target block, on the opposite side to the redstone dust. Add a solid block on top of all the redstone torches and another row of solid blocks on the inside of the target blocks, with redstone dust on top.

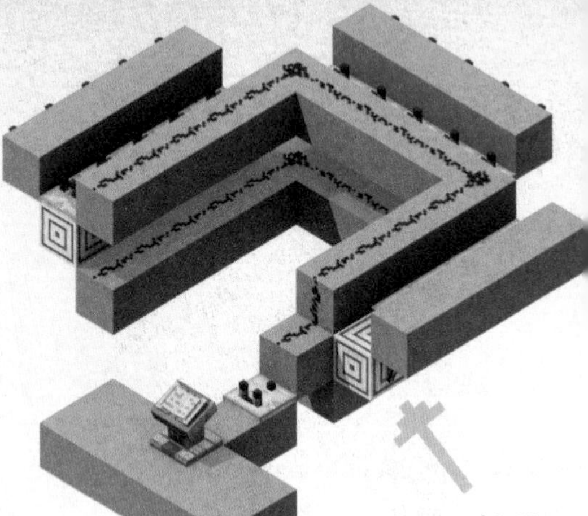

Place a redstone torch here and on the outside of every target block, all the way round.

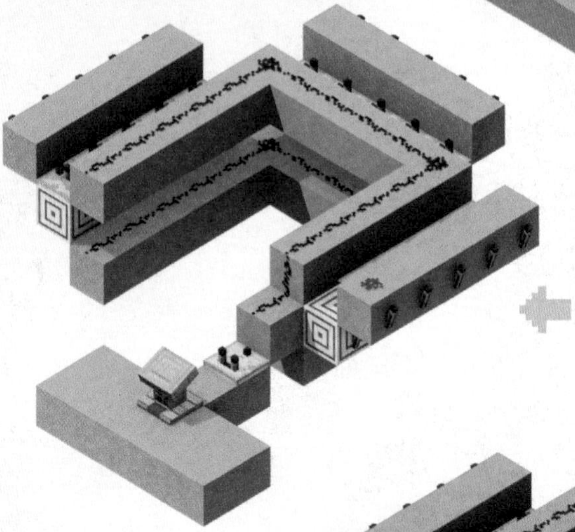

5 Now you need to add a redstone torch on the front of those blocks you just placed around the outside. Also add redstone dust on top of the block with the first torch.

6 Create a new row of solid blocks beside the single redstone dust you just placed. Add 2 solid blocks towards the centre of the build, then place a concrete slab beside them. Now add 3 more solid blocks in an L formation, pointing into the centre of the build. Add redstone dust along the top of this new row.

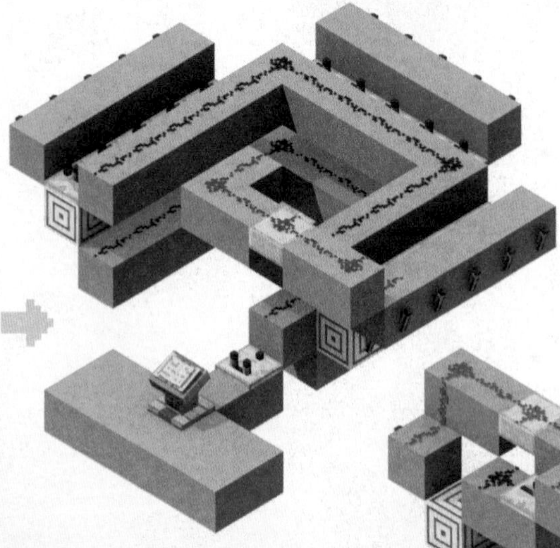

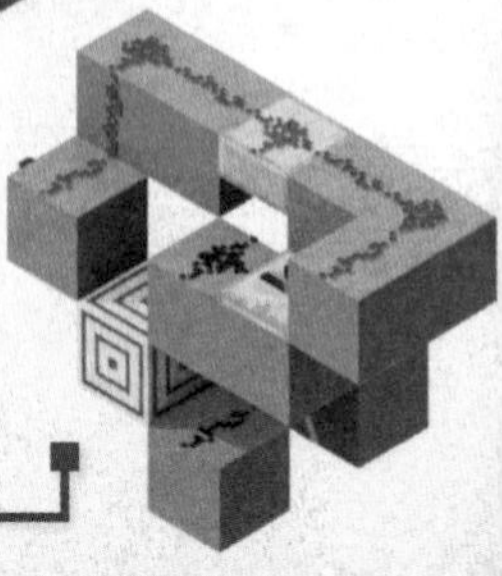

REVERSE DETAIL VIEW

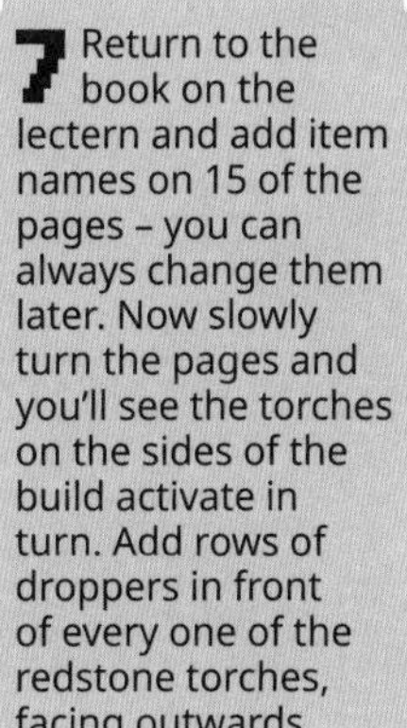

7 Return to the book on the lectern and add item names on 15 of the pages – you can always change them later. Now slowly turn the pages and you'll see the torches on the sides of the build activate in turn. Add rows of droppers in front of every one of the redstone torches, facing outwards.

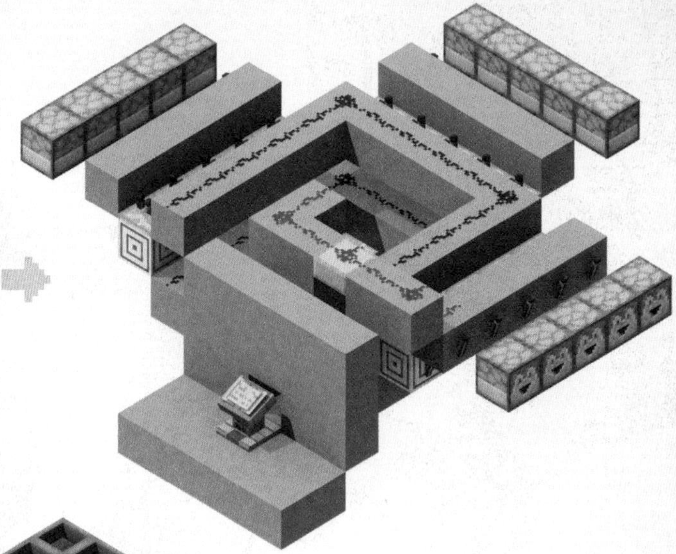

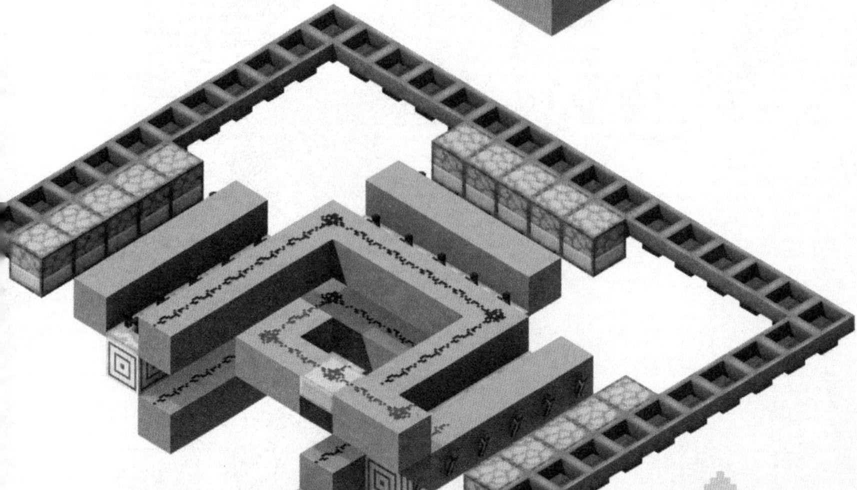

8 Starting in front of the dropper at the end of the left-hand row, add a hopper that has an output tube facing clockwise. Add hoppers running around all three sides of the droppers as shown in the image, coming to an end within one blocks alignment of the lectern. Check the final hopper's output tube faces the lectern, too.

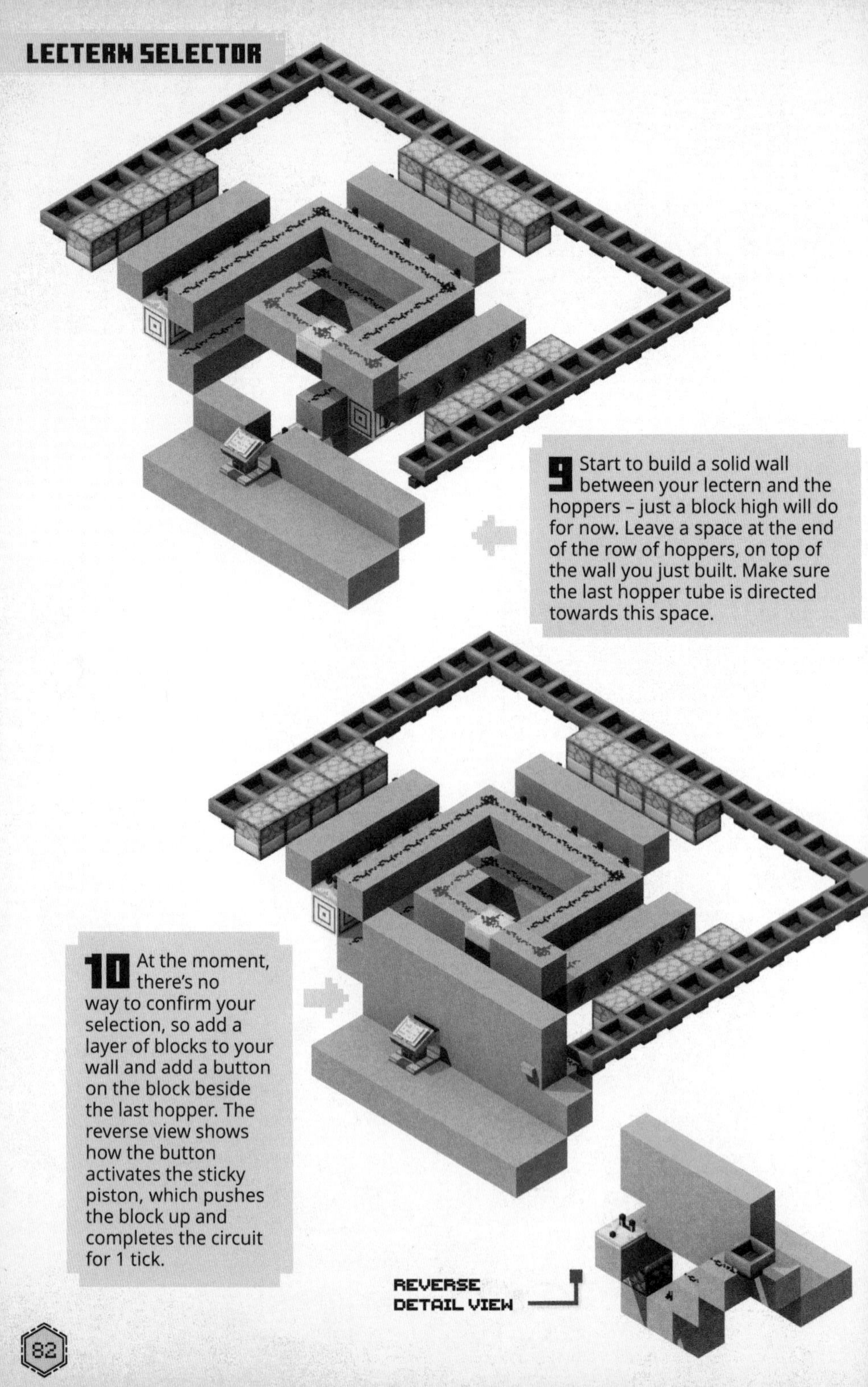

9 Start to build a solid wall between your lectern and the hoppers – just a block high will do for now. Leave a space at the end of the row of hoppers, on top of the wall you just built. Make sure the last hopper tube is directed towards this space.

10 At the moment, there's no way to confirm your selection, so add a layer of blocks to your wall and add a button on the block beside the last hopper. The reverse view shows how the button activates the sticky piston, which pushes the block up and completes the circuit for 1 tick.

11 Disguise the blocks around the space by building an intricate stone wall. This will help make the space appear as a simple hole in the wall.

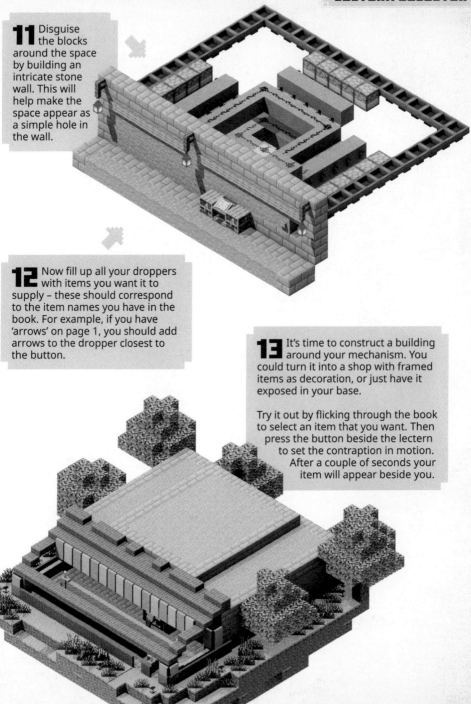

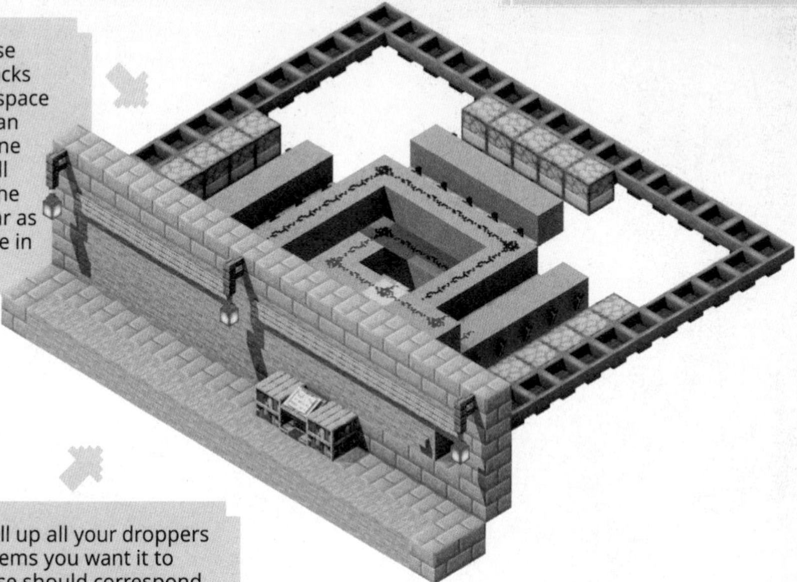

12 Now fill up all your droppers with items you want it to supply – these should correspond to the item names you have in the book. For example, if you have 'arrows' on page 1, you should add arrows to the dropper closest to the button.

13 It's time to construct a building around your mechanism. You could turn it into a shop with framed items as decoration, or just have it exposed in your base.

Try it out by flicking through the book to select an item that you want. Then press the button beside the lectern to set the contraption in motion. After a couple of seconds your item will appear beside you.

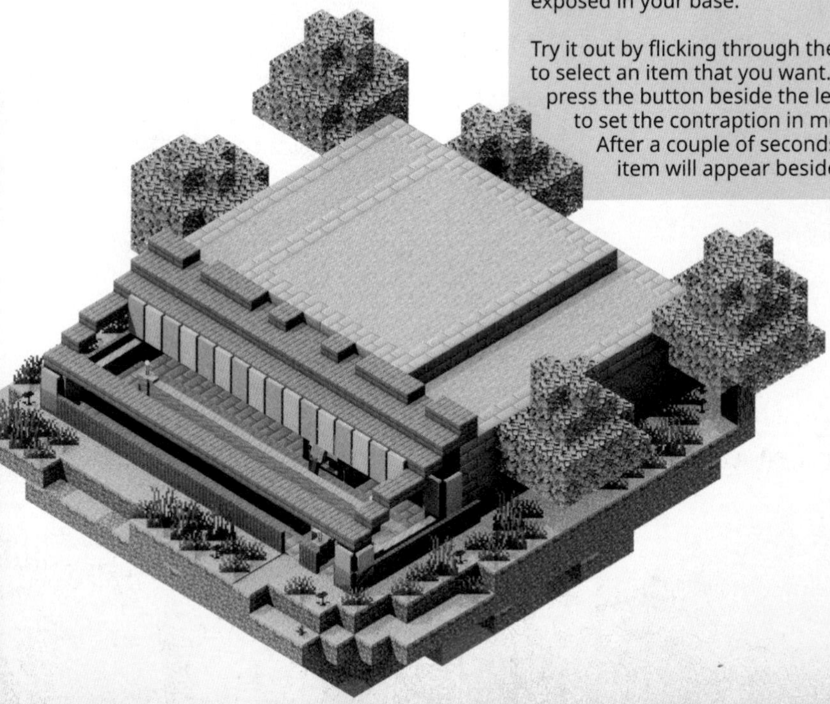

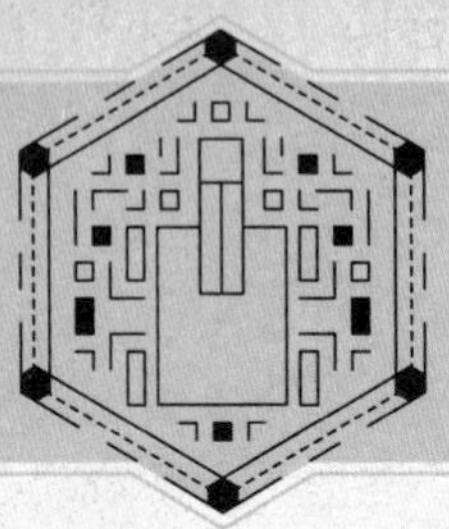

ALTERNATIVE SELECTORS

SMALLER SELECTOR

This is perfect if you like the idea of a lectern selector but don't have the time for a big build, or if you'd like to fit a selector system into an existing base. Using the same mechanics, you can create a smaller contraption that works in a similar way. Follow the steps for our lectern selector, but use just one straight line of droppers and hoppers.

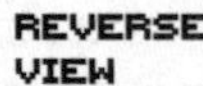

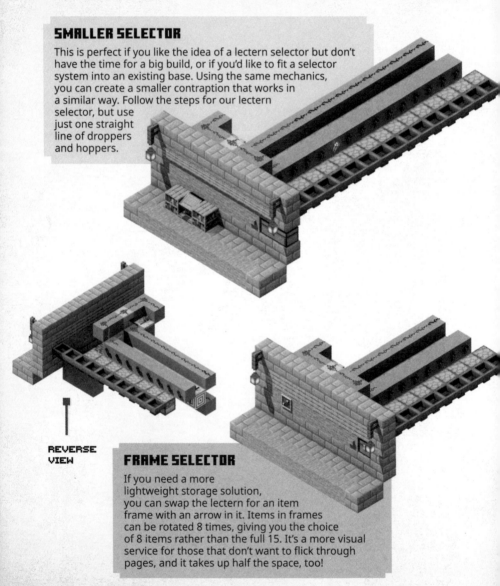

REVERSE VIEW

FRAME SELECTOR

If you need a more lightweight storage solution, you can swap the lectern for an item frame with an arrow in it. Items in frames can be rotated 8 times, giving you the choice of 8 items rather than the full 15. It's a more visual service for those that don't want to flick through pages, and it takes up half the space, too!

There are so many possibilities with the mechanism of the selector build. You can use it to measure different items, collect a whole inventory's worth of items in storage, or go all out and catalogue every single item in Minecraft. Here are some alternative selector ideas.

MASS PRODUCTION

By changing the button that links the item dropper to a lever and adding a clock circuit after the lectern, you can make the circuit trigger repeatedly dispense multiples of the same item. There's no simple way to choose an exact number, but this will be a great addition if you want a full inventory of arrows, decorative blocks and foods.

DETAILED VIEW

ITEM LIBRARY

For those of you that like to be VERY organised, consider creating an item library. This is basically the build repeated over and over again, with a dispenser for every single block in the game, so you will always have EVERY block at your disposal. Add signage to the front of each lectern selector for easy reference – bonus points if you alphabetise the items – and stairs to navigate the various levels.

TEACHING REDSTONE WITH: JIGARBOV

WHY TEACH REDSTONE?

'I made Jig's Guide: Redstone Basics because I just love redstone. It's one of things that elevates your interactions with the world from merely mining, surviving and building to puzzle-solving, creating automated solutions and being able to create contraptions that have an impact on the world around you, outside of your regular pickaxe.'

DID YOU SEE A NEED FOR REDSTONE LESSONS?

'I don't necessarily think it's a problem for people, but I do consider it intimidating to start. There are a lot of different components and it can be difficult to know where to begin. Players often have an easy time exploring and discovering how to overcome different challenges in Minecraft, but redstone isn't one that immediately presents itself since there are almost no instructions on how to actually use any of it.'

HOW DOES IT COMPARE TO HOW YOU LEARNT?

'When I started, there were very few sources of information aside from a few YouTube videos. I wish I had something like this when I started out, so I hope everyone gives it a try, gets some experience and sees that redstone isn't as scary as it looks, but if you're reading this book, you already know that!'

Not content with just being a master engineer, our resident redstone expert Jigarbov is also intent on spreading his knowledge to the wider community. With his free Marketplace creation, Jig's Guide: Redstone Basics, he's getting more people into redstone in an exciting way.

WHAT DO YOU TEACH THAT MINECRAFT DOESN'T?

'Lots of people use external sources to help learn about various Minecraft mechanics, this book included. They give a wonderful overview of the different things you can do in the game, but by the nature of the medium, there is that separation since you are not hands-on. Redstone in particular is one of those tough things to learn without directly getting your hands dirty. My hope with Jig's Guide, is that through the introductory lessons, you can get your hands dirty without the roadblock of not knowing where to start.'

WHAT IS THE END GOAL?

'By the end of the basic lessons in Jig's Guide, I would hope players have a good understanding of the fundamentals. Things like how far redstone can transmit power, things that can be used to power it and what kind of things can be triggered by it. Each component also has a room dedicated to it and is being updated each time a new redstone item is added, so that players can learn about them and interact with them in a way that they feel emboldened to experiment on their own.'

WILL IT MAKE YOU A REDSTONE MASTER?

'I'm not sure anyone is ever a redstone master! Even I am learning new things every day. There are some slightly more complicated machines in the map that are signposted with how they work. The hope is that players see what is possible and that they learn enough to get started on their journey to discovering the full potential of redstone and not just opening a door.'

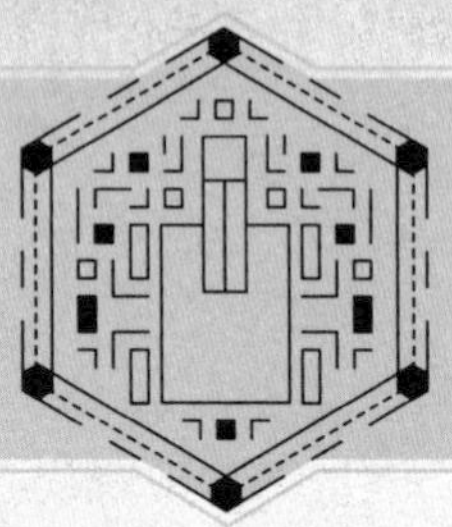

TUNNEL BORER

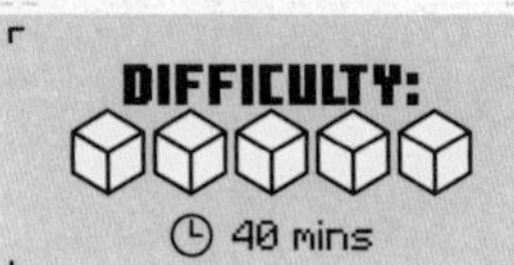

MAIN BLOCKS

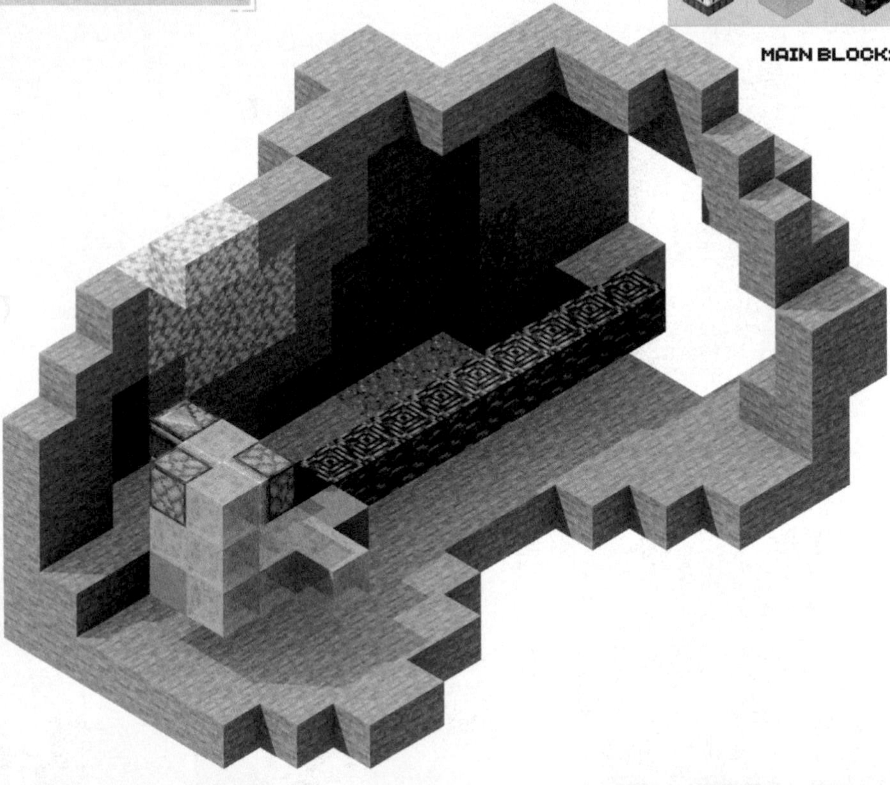

FRONT

SIDE

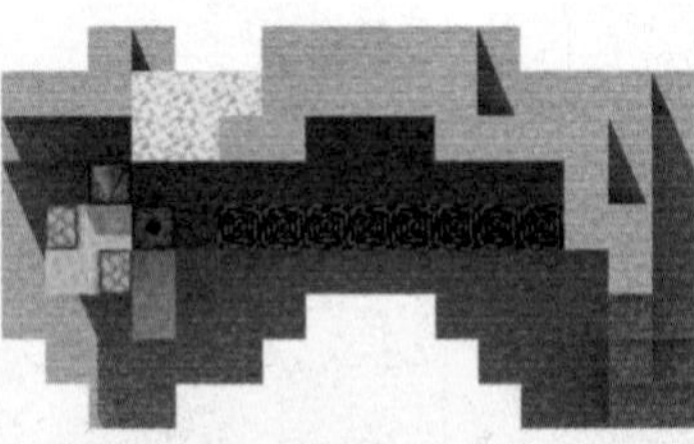
TOP

If you want to simplify the mining process, then this tunnel borer is the perfect build for you. It uses a dispenser to prime and launch TNT from a redstone mech that inches forward with every explosion. Follow these steps and you'll be mining with ease in no time.

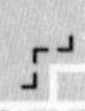

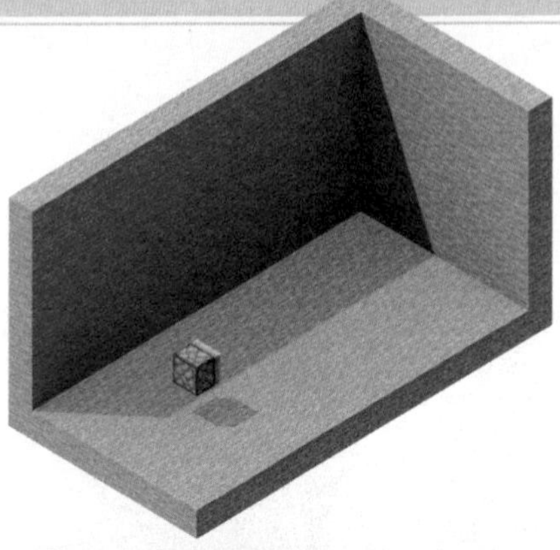

1 Dig down into the ground and excavate a space that's 7 blocks wide, 7 blocks tall and 15 blocks long. Place a piston facing in the direction that you want your borer to travel, 3 blocks away from both walls and 1 block above the floor.

2 Behind the piston, place an observer. It's observing face should be pointing away from the piston, so the output face is pointing into it. Put another observer on top of it, facing in the opposite direction.

3 Place a dispenser on top of the piston, with its output face facing up. This is where you will place the TNT. The dispenser will push out and activate the TNT – but don't add it yet or you could blow up your contraption.

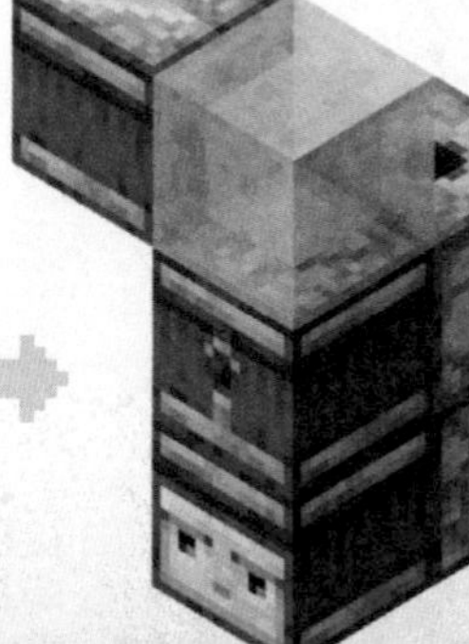

4 Put a slime block on top of the second observer, then add another observer to one side, facing away from the slime block. You might need to place a couple of temporary blocks in order to get it to face the right way.

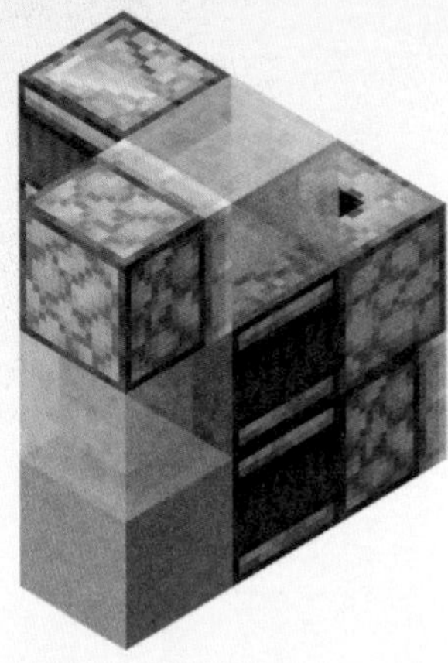

5 Put a solid block behind the bottom observer from step 3, then top that with another slime block and a piston facing your first slime block. This piston will push the slime when activated, causing the TNT to travel away from the contraption.

6 Place a sticky piston to the right of the topmost slime block, facing the back of your contraption. Attach a slime block to its face, then create an L-shape of slime blocks from there, so the L ends just beside the bottom sticky piston.

7 Add a solid block in front of the last slime block, and an extra slime block to the right side of that slime.

If you make the ancient debris column any smaller, it's likely to destroy your mechanism.

8 In front of the piston that's beneath the dispenser, leave a block space and then add a line of nine ancient debris. These are resistant to TNT blasts like obsidian, but can be pushed and pulled by slime and pistons.

9 Excavate the ground beneath and around the tunnel borer to make sure that no blocks are accidentally attached to the sticky slime in the build. If they are, then it will exceed a piston's push limit and break the borer.

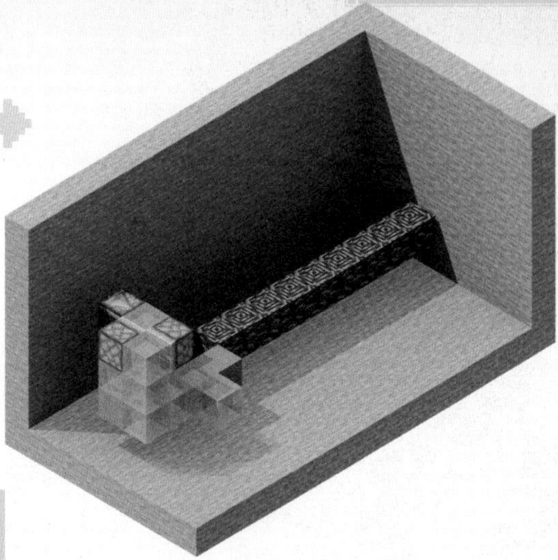

10 Now fill the dispenser with TNT and place a button on the side of it. When you press it, it will dispense the TNT, which the observers will detect and power the pistons that are around them. This will launch the TNT down the line of ancient debris and push the slime forward, dragging everything with it.

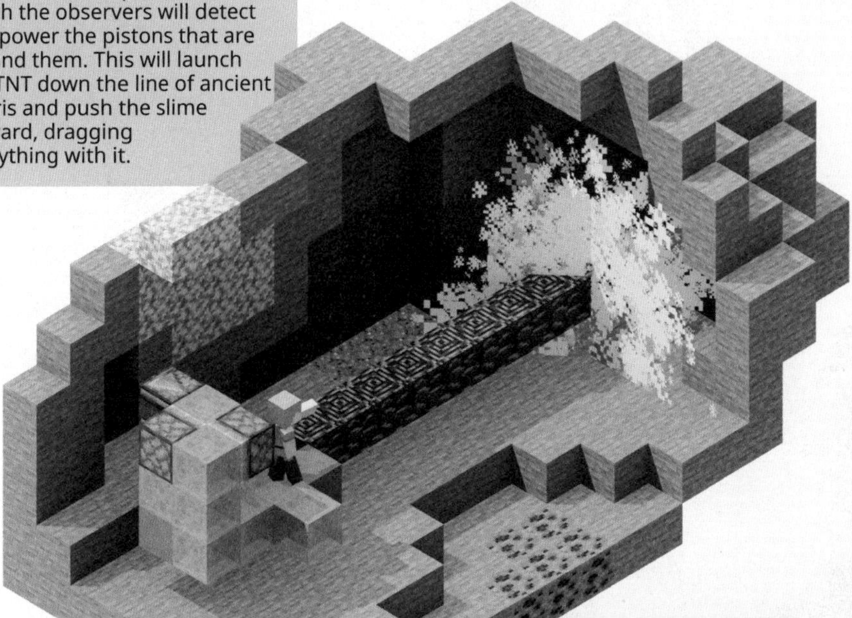

TOP TIP

The button will be destroyed by the movement when you press it as it's not attached to slime or a sticky piston, but you can pick it up, place it and press again to keep the borer moving.

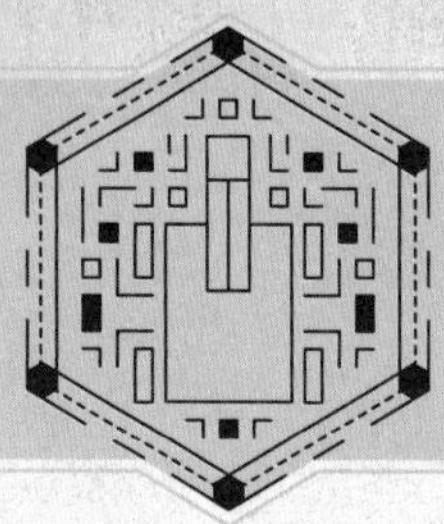

MORE MOVING MECHANISMS

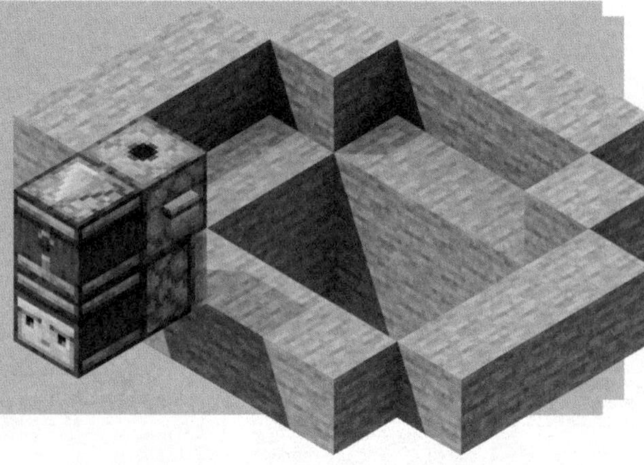

STATIC MINER

The combination of slime, pistons and observers can be whittled down so that the contraption only fires off the TNT and doesn't move along with it. Rather than creating horizontal tunnels, you'll create gigantic chasms that lead all the way down to the bedrock level. As it doesn't move, the button will stay in place, too.

You need a longer clock to ensure that the TNT has a chance to detonate before launching a new block.

REPEATING POWER

If you can keep the button in place, that also means that you can automate the system further. Replace the button on the static miner with a long-delay clock circuit to launch a TNT block every couple of seconds – those precious seconds allow the TNT to land and explode before any more is launched. You might need to rebuild once the chasm is lower than around 80 blocks though, as TNT won't hit the floor anymore!

With the tunnel borer, we've seen what you can do to automate the mining process, but the possibilities don't end there. Using similar methods, you can create static mining devices such as a TNT launcher, and other moving vehicles ... even a rocket!

PLANES, TRAINS AND ... ROCKETS

The moving mechanism contained in the borer is quite complex, but shows that moving machines are possible. This simplified contraption uses the same blocks – observers, pistons and slime blocks – to create automatic movement that can be a good base for experimentation and expansion. You can even craft one vertically to make a rocket!

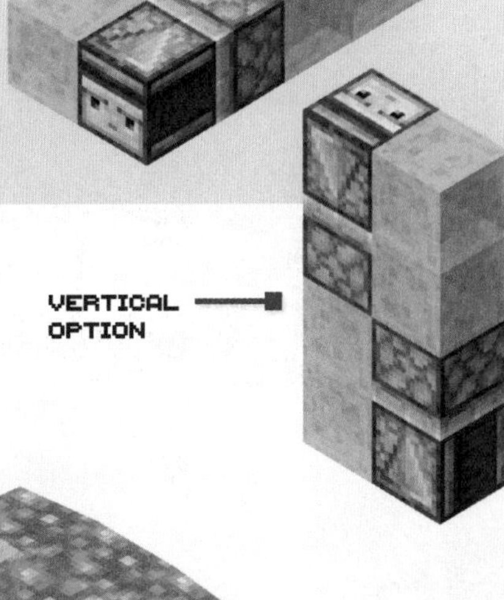

MATERIAL CREATOR

If you turn the dispenser around to face forwards instead of up (you can also get rid of the piston that pushes the TNT), you can use this contraption for other means. Fill the dispenser with buckets of water and as it travels over lava, it will create cobblestone blocks – or obsidian if it hits lava source blocks. If you pour lava over water instead, you can make stone. There are plenty of other things you can dispense to adapt the contraption to your needs, too.

Lava can also create basalt when above soul soil and touching blue ice.

GOODBYE

Did you know that Redstone was the name for the rockets that took the first American astronauts into space? These wonders of engineering were the product of the exact same kind of thinking that you've been doing as you've read and played your way through this book.

You've learned how simple components can come together to produce complex results, and you've probably learned how to solve problems when they don't work as you expect, too!

So what's next? You can take it even further by watching videos produced by other redstone engineers. Remember that everyone, even the creators of Minecraft's adventure maps and mini games, started just like you!

And never underestimate what you can learn simply by playing around for yourself. Tinker; experiment; break it; fix it: project by project, you'll find yourself becoming a redstone expert.

THANKS FOR PLAYING!

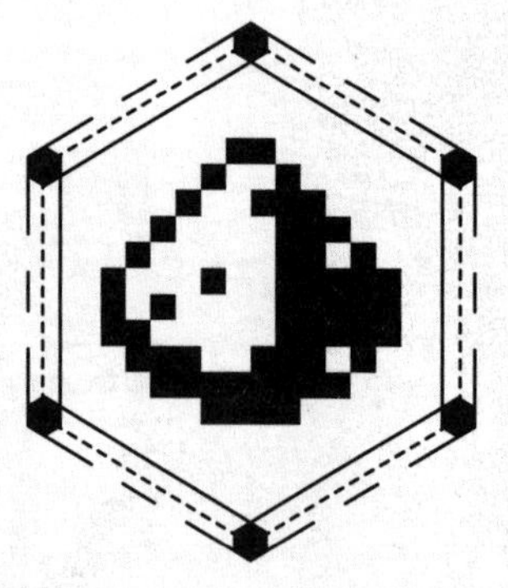

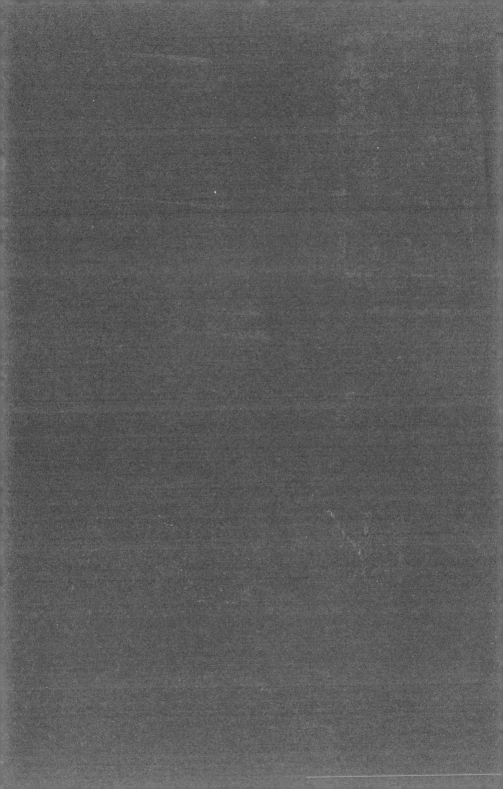